ENDORSEMENTS

Read *Quit Pastoring Your Church* and explore the "crazy calling" of planting a church in Christ's Kingdom. Let it grip you with the vision of the impossible task made possible when "Jesus is pastor." Allow Aaron Gerrard to disrupt your best agendas, paint you a new picture, and reset expectations so that Jesus can become the very real living center of life and ministry in this thing we call church.

— **DAVID FITCH,**
professor at Northern Seminary
author of *Faithful Presence*

Quit Pastoring Your Church offers a tantalizing vision for ministry done in the Spirit of Jesus. This book is bracingly honest, spiritually informed, and theologically engaged as it untangles our (not so) subtle control over our own pastoral work and guides toward Jesus, our Pastor. Gerrard offers hope for ministering persons of all stripes to discover the life-giving reality of pastoral ministry practiced in intimate communion with the Father, Son and Holy Spirit.

— **JIM HORSTHUIS,**
Academic Director
Pathways School of Ministry

Quit Pastoring Your Church is an honest look at the life of a pastor. It's an inspiring story of one person who wades his way through pain and suffering and personal crisis and encounters Jesus in the midst of it. As I read it, I was challenged by Aaron's commitment to live by his principles, and encouraged by the work that God has been doing in his life and in his church. Aaron confronts some of the standard practices of evangelical churches, particularly, decision making, focusing on numerical growth, and minimizing the importance of sacramental practices, and invites us to rethink what our practices reveal about what we value and believe. He winsomely invites us to engage in the courageous journey of following Jesus as Lead Pastor.

— MARDI DOLFO-SMITH,
Discipleship Pastor
North Shore Alliance Church

We could all claim that we recognize that Jesus is the head of the church. But would anyone know that to be true if the average local church was the only corroborating evidence for our claims? Aaron Gerard has done something important with this book. He has made practical something that many of us only conceive of theoretically. You're about to read the story of how a church has made Jesus their pastor. I consider this book to be essential reading for anyone considering a call to pastoral ministry or for the myriad of pastors and churches that face the ongoing temptation to let just about everything and everyone but Jesus lead.

— JARED SIEBERT,
Director of Church Planting
Free Methodist Church in Canada

quit pastoring your church.

quit pastoring your church.

**The story of
a small church
making Jesus
their pastor**

AARON D. GERRARD

© 2020 New Leaf Network Press.

publishing@newleafnetwork.ca
newleafnetwork.ca

435 Kingsmere Blvd,
Saskatoon, SK S7J 3T9

Aaron D. Gerrard
Quit Pastoring Your Church.

Cover & Layout by: Regan Neudorf

Photography by: Krista Jefferson (www.edisonphotography.com)

Scripture quotations in this publication are from the Common English Bible, unless otherwise noted, .

© Copyright 2011 by the Common English Bible. All rights reserved. Used by permission.

New Revised Standard Version of the Bible, copyright 1989 by the Division of Christian Education of the National Council of Churches of Christ in the USA. Used by permission. All rights reserved.

ISBN: 978-0-9953054-2-7

CONTENTS

Foreword by Lee Beach
Dedication & Thanks
Introduction

The Need for Something Different

1. The Wall
2. Do We Believe Jesus is Alive, Can Speak, & Lead?

How to Try Something Different

3. Who Are Your Prophets?
4. Of Robert & Discernment
5. Can Jesus Lead You to Consensus?
6. New Models for Leadership

New Expectations

7. The Table
8. A New Unity
9. The Bible
10. Nurturing a Life with *the* Pastor: Selected Stories

Conclusion

FOREWARD
by Lee Beach

"In eight years together, we have never taken a congregational vote. We have never, ever voted on anything. We function on a model that seeks to discern the voice of Jesus in our midst so that we can come to consensus around any decisions that we have to make." This was quite a shock to most of the students in the classroom that day. I am a seminary professor, and I was talking to my class about my own local church, *Ancaster Village Church* (AVC) in the wonderful village of Ancaster on the west end of the great city of Hamilton, ON, Canada. We were discussing how to plant a church and I was suggesting that when you plant a church you need to make sure that Jesus is the pastor of the church. This was a bit disorienting to my poor students. They were clearly struggling to understand what that means. Beside me at the front of the class that day, serving as a guest lecturer was my pastor, and good friend Aaron Gerrard. He had spent the last few minutes talking about this idea that Jesus really needs to be the pastor of every church, and that new church starts have the unique opportunity to form a congregation that takes this concept seriously. There seemed to be enthusiasm around the idea, but there was also confusion about how that worked in practice and some skepticism as to whether it was realistic as a leadership model. While I truly understood the students' hesitancy in embracing this idea, I also stood there that bright Spring morning knowing that what Aaron and I were presenting can actually work. Jesus really can be the pastor of your church, and this book will help show you how.

Throughout these pages Aaron offers us an attempt to reimagine the pastoral office by taking seriously the idea that Jesus, through the presence of his spirit, genuinely wants to guide and direct his church. It captures the teaching Jesus offered to his disciples that the Spirit would "guide you into all truth, for he will not speak on his own, but will speak whatever he hears, and he will declare to you the things that are to come... he will take what is mine and declare it to you." (John 16:13-15 NRSV) This is a key idea in scripture that we often under emphasize or even ignore. I have been involved in several churches, both as a lay leader and pastor. Each of these congregations took prayer seriously and would not make plans or major decisions without asking for God's guidance first. However, in those congregations I also experienced the reality of different people, or groups of people coming to opposing conclusions on things and the inevitable vote that took place would leave some people feeling ostracized, unheard and wounded. I understand that this is sometimes unavoidable in human relationships, even in the most well-meaning church congregation, but I could not help but feel there was a better way to do things. It wasn't just about whether to take a vote or not, that is not really the main issue, it was about how we related to Jesus as our true leader and then how that should affect how we relate to one another. What does it mean when the author of 1 Peter exhorts elders in the church to tend the flock with integrity so that "when the chief shepherd appears you will win the crown of glory that never fades away." (see 1 Peter 5:1-4 NRSV) What does it mean that Jesus is the chief shepherd? Is this just a metaphor, or a throw away thought that the author offers? Or is this a theological concept that deserves to be understood and implemented? This book is an exploration of what it might look like for a church to reflect deeply on the idea that Jesus is the real pastor, not in some absentee landlord kind of a way, but in a way that is meaningful in the daily life of the congregation.

As Gerrard helps us explore this concept and all its implications on life together as a church, he honestly addresses many of the traditional mindsets that are intrinsic to church life in general and the evangelical tradition in particular. Some of the foibles and failings that he highlights will be familiar to anyone who has hung around the church long enough. Some may make you uncomfortable, others will make you smile in recognition. If we are honest, most of us have been culpable in perpetuating some of the behaviours that have not always served the church well. Along the way we will be reminded of the book that sometimes functions like a second bible in church governance, *Roberts Rules of Order*. Aaron reminds us of all the "joys" it brings to congregational decision making and how it can be used in a way that deters from truly engaging in listening to the Spirit. On a more positive note, Aaron calls us to learn the art of communal theological reflection, to learn how to employ Ignation spirituality as an approach to congregational decision making, and to learn the value of waiting on God and exercising patience with both him and the people we are forming missional community with.

None of this is purely theory. All of this is rooted in the real life of *Ancaster Village Church*. I have been a part of this congregation and its unfolding journey since its inception. I was there for the very first meeting, as Aaron describes in the book, a little more than twenty of us shoehorned into Aaron and Shay's family room. That night we first discussed what it might look like to do church a little differently than most of us had experienced it. As we continued to meet and dream, we discussed what it would look like to be a church that was committed to listening to the Spirit. What would it look like for us to truly respect one another's insights and to wait on each other if that was what was needed? Could we find a process of discernment that enabled us to practice genuine listening to God and one another? Was it possible for Jesus to truly be our pastor? Over the years together we have had to learn things, we have had awkward moments and a few missteps along the way. We are far from perfect. As a small collective of Jesus followers we are spectacularly unspectacular, as normal and flawed as can be. But we have always managed to find consensus. Most of the people who were present in the very early days are still together, still on the same journey, glad that some others have joined us along the way. We work and struggle together to be a church that embodies the good news of the gospel for the sake of the community around us.

While Aaron states that this book is primarily designed to be for pastors, don't believe him. While it is definitely an invaluable resource for pastors and church planters, it will inspire your imagination and draw you to Jesus no matter what role you play (or do not play) in your local church. It is a book that at its core is spiritual theology. It is rooted in deep, reflective Christian theology, but also invites you to practice spiritual disciplines that give theology its life. It is cerebral but full of heart. Good for any of us who wants to take being led by Jesus seriously.

In the end the book reminds us that things don't have to be the same in the church in the years ahead. In fact, they must not be. In an increasingly Post-Christian Western society we desperately need to reconceive how the church should function. There are different ways to think and different ways to practice faith together and this book recovers an ancient idea, rooted in scripture, and presents it in a way that allows us to think about congregational life in fresh and generative new ways. Things do not have to be the same, you just have to let Jesus be your pastor.

LEE BEACH

Associate Professor of Christian Ministry,
McMaster Divinity College

DEDICATION & THANKS

This must begin with my parents.

I grew up in the church. Both my mom and dad have been neck deep in church leadership my whole life. From the moment of my first breath my parents have modelled a life of service, investment, and sacrifice in the church. My dad was a pastor for decades before moving into executive roles within our denomination. My mom was sometimes a pastor, always involved in some leadership capacity, and is now also in an executive role within our denomination. But these have never been just jobs for my parents; they have been life-encompassing. And that has been a good thing. I owe so much of my love of the church to my parents. Their service to the church and their hope in what the church can do in the world through Jesus is something that has formed and encouraged me — in so many ways it has made me who I am. I grew up sitting around the dinner table long after our meals were over listening to my mom and dad talk about church stuff with their friends, peers, other leaders in the church, missionaries on their way through, and neighbours. Many of my extended family are also involved in church ministry so their visits were another time for me to sit and listen to all of the shop talk and denominational scuttlebutt. And while I have friends who grew up in similar situations and felt their experience hurt or hindered their own faith, my experience was just the opposite. My parents, no matter what was going on in their own ministries and despite all of the hurts and frustrations that came with church, always demonstrated grace, faith, and hope. Words cannot express how much I love my parents, am proud of them, and how much I owe them for how they raised me to understand and value the local church.

It is important that I begin by saying that because when you write a book like this — a book which deconstructs and critiques many embedded beliefs and structures — it would be easy to think that I have no use for so much of what I observed and was taught by my parents and, really, their generation of leaders. That is simply not true. It is their faith, hope, service, and belief in the church's good purposes that have not only helped in keeping me around, but also pushed me to believe even more for the church. It is my parent's ministry that has enabled my own. It is the conversations I overhead them have with family and friends about how they wanted something better for their churches and our denomination that inspire me to do the same. So to Doug and Glendyne, this book is a tribute to you. I dedicate it to you. Thank-you.

I must also acknowledge my sisters, Karmyn and Lauryl, who have patiently put up with me their whole lives. I am grateful to be your brother and friend, proud of you both, and thankful for your wonderful families. I wish you both lived closer.

There are so many people to thank that this task feels more daunting than that of completing the book. Thanks to Lee for writing the forward and for being a friend and mentor. It is hard to imagine my ministry without yours to me. Thanks to the many who read a version of this book and offered advice, critique, and the encouragement to finish the project. To those who wrote endorsements, your thoughtful words and the time you invested mean a great deal to me. Regan, for all the work you put in . . . you have a gift.

To Jared, Amy, and all my friends at New Leaf, thanks for your friendship and support. Our church and this project are a direct result of the good things New Leaf does for dreamers, dreams, and the hope of the Good News in Canada. Thank you for investing in this project, for believing in it, and for seeing it through. I have learned so much from all of you. You are my peers and friends in the crazy belief that Jesus wins and his church gets to be a part of that. I am honoured to be a part of what you are doing in this country.

I owe my denomination gratitude. Without it and its influence on my life I would not have met so many of the amazing people who have shaped my faith and ministry. *The Christian and Missionary Alliance in Canada* is home to many good people who love Jesus and serve his church. These people cared for me and educated me while growing up, while at *Canadian Bible College* in Regina, SK, during my first pastorate in Surrey, B.C., and on the list goes. My connection to the C&MA has given me a wealth of experiences and relationships for which I am so grateful.

To Daniel, Chris, and Jon, your friendships have for years been a lifeline, a sounding board, a place of correction and critique, an encouragement, and have also provided great comedy and lasting memories. No one can rant like we do. And yet those rants have inspired so much hope and perseverance in my life that it is hard to quantify just how valuable they have been. You guys are my iron sharpeners. Thank-you.

Ancaster Village Church. You have been a gift of God's grace to me and my family. You have provided the space and environment for me to be me. You may not realize it, but for a pastor that is a very special and rare thing. I am simply me, and you accept and support me. I never feel like I need to be a superstar, like I need to hide my shortfalls, or like I need to be anyone else. Thank-you. I wish every pastor had a home like I do. Thanks for the time to make this project happen. And thanks for being the guinea pigs to see if any of this stuff actually works.

Finally, my family.

To Shalene, Jaxton, Ryah, and Brit, I love you all so much. I married *way* up, Redhead. You are my favourite. I cannot imagine this journey without you. And kids, you are okay, too.

INTRODUCTION

A couple of times a year I get to work with men and women who are considering starting a new church. We call it a *Design Shop*. It is a project of the *New Leaf Network*, a collaborative group of Christian leaders from a broad spectrum of denominations. These people are working to help the Canadian Church discover new potential, with new conversations, new leaders, and new initiatives. Some attendees participate with merely an emerging idea and a sense of new purpose, some have started a project, and some are far enough along into an initiative that they are starting to question their sanity. Regardless of where a person fits, these are my favourite people to hang out with. They are dreamers, risk-takers, and innovators. In the face of our current culture and many of the obstacles therein, these people are willing to try. Something. Anything. It may be something that lasts a while. It may be something that ends quickly. But they are going to push forward. And I love it.

Over the years that I have been attending this event I have noticed one common denominator. For those who are going to take a risk and give it a shot, they are united by an inescapable feeling that Jesus is asking them to take it. Somehow, their unique journey through life has led them to this moment, and with great fear, trembling, and excitement, they are listening to Jesus say, "Let's *do* this." They cling to this idea that Jesus is asking them to join him in something. I am fascinated by this shared experience because the same thing happened to me, and to be in a room with others who have embraced this sort of crazy calling is deeply affirming.

Throughout our time together in the *Design Shop* we discuss many of the obstacles and realities leaders of new churches will face and will need to be attuned to: culture shifts and trends, a lack of funding, missional awareness within particular contexts, a lack of funding, spiritual attacks, strains on a leader's family, a lack of funding, apathy or antagonism within culture, and many other challenges that to a normal person would be enough to say, "Forget it." Did I mention a lack of funding? But new church leaders are atypical. In the church planting world we refer to these people as those who have accepted and said yes to the "collect call" from God. They are a bit strange, crazy even. They do not wait complacently for God to open doors; they kick them down!
I am allowed to call them strange because I am one of these people. About eight years ago I discerned my "collect call" and became haunted by the inescapable feeling that Jesus was asking me start a church. I knew nothing about what I was getting myself into. I had never planted a church before. Though I had previously been a pastor in a traditional mid-sized Evangelical

church, very little of that skill-set and knowledge prepared me for the days ahead.

Before starting my work as a church planter I attended the *Design Shop*. It was so helpful and inspiring that I took it again as a refresher course a few years into my church's new life. Soon after that I was asked to come on board as one of the instructors. I agreed, but on one condition: I wanted to develop a new session about the centrality of Jesus. Thankfully, whenever you phrase something like that, you make it extremely difficult for someone to reply with a "no." My idea was accepted and now, among other things, I conclude the *Design Shop* by teaching a session I entitled, "Jesus as Pastor."

As I mentioned, the unifying characteristic of the attendees of a *Design Shop* is that they cannot escape the sense that Jesus is asking them to try something new. Without fail, when someone is asked to share their story regarding how they ended up at the *Design Shop*, they will share a deep, moving, and powerfully intimate testimony of how Jesus stepped into their life, made himself known, and asked them to take a risk. "Jesus put this place on my heart." "Jesus said he needed me to introduce him to that group of people." These are the sorts of statements you hear, and throughout our time together the instructors consistently remind the attendees never to forget those experiences. Why? Because there will be a day, a week, a month, a year, maybe longer, when those stories will be all there is to hold onto. In the face of adversity — in the darkest of days — all you may have is your story that Jesus is real and asked you to take this risk. "Jesus as Pastor" is a session I developed especially to make this point. As new church leaders there are — and will be — many days we need to be reminded that we once had a conversation with Jesus accepting a risk to follow him into uncharted territory.

What this common experience speaks to, emphatically so, is that this is a journey *with* Jesus. It is not a journey that ends after the "collect call" is made and accepted. At least it should not be. I have mentioned that my church planting journey began when Jesus asked me to do something. What I have come to learn is that he did not ask me to do something without him, but rather to partner *with* him. His request was not merely the seed of an idea, but instead an invitation to adventure with him.

Reflecting on my own ministry experiences, and after having chatted with many of my pastor friends and peers, I became soundly aware of the second — though not lesser — purpose behind teaching the "Jesus as Pastor" session. The journey of pastoral ministry is one of understanding, giving way to, and following the real-time pastoral leadership of Jesus in our local church. It has been a years long process of learning how to quit pastoring my church in place of giving leadership to Jesus.

Jesus is real. He is with you. He is for you. He is your pastor. And he wants you to lead your church with more than a memory that he asked you to do so. Instead, he wants you to lead your church by letting *him* lead it. He wants you to quit pastoring your church. "Jesus as Pastor" was developed as a way of discussing this in inspirational, anecdotal, practical, and theological terms. This concept reimagines the pastoral office in today's local church.

My problem with teaching this session at the *Design Shop* was that I only have 45 minutes to unpack it. Which is why I find myself here, writing a book. This book is what I wish I could say in my 45 minute session.

Perhaps you are thinking these statements — "Jesus is real. He is with you. He is for you. He is your pastor. And he wants to be the pastor of your church." — are obvious. By most people's definition of evangelicalism Jesus is key to our theology, our understanding of salvation, and the lens through which we make sense of creation. Yet many of my observations and experiences while growing up in Evangelical churches, and throughout a career of pastoring within them, have led me to believe that we do not believe those things in real time. My experience within the Evangelical church, which promotes a Jesus-centric view on paper, is paper-thin in practice. I have wondered, did I miss something? Am I alone in perceiving this gap between belief and practice? But the more I have shared the following ideas, stories, and practices with others in ministry, the more evident it has become that this is a much-needed discussion within Evangelicalism. This may, for some in pastoral leadership, simply be a helpful way to put some language and reference to practices already in place. For others, evaluating Jesus as pastor anew may be more challenging, exciting, and provocative.

So here we are. This is my "Jesus as Pastor" session, the long version.

Foremost, this is a church planter's confessional. This is me being honest with you about many things I have learned, failed at, and hope to keep figuring out. Therefore, if you are thinking about starting a new church or are in the process of starting a new church, this book is for you. More broadly, I hope this book will be useful to anyone in local church pastoral ministry, an invitation to be brave about what church really takes. Of course, anyone is welcome to read on, but I am writing as a pastor to pastors. And while I have experience in established, more traditional, local church settings, most of what I am discussing within these pages comes from a church planting context. While that means it may resonate more with those with the same experience in church planting, I do believe everything is transferable to established churches. I also admit up front that as a member of the Evangelical club, I feel free to critique, deconstruct, and operate with a bit of sarcasm regarding my own tradition. Admittedly, if you cannot laugh at yourself and your own tradition, this book may not be for you. I certainly hope to offer ideas of reconstruction, too.

To begin I will try to set the stage (as you will see, I use this metaphor intentionally) with a theology of the pastoral office. What am I as a pastor, and what am I not? If it is Jesus who is to pastor me and my church, it is paramount that I begin by getting this theology correct. From there I will move into a space which hopefully provokes you to think on what it is you believe about Jesus. Where is he? What can he do? What does he want to do? If you can come out of that discussion believing that there is something unique about him, then I offer several suggestions through the following chapters regarding how to practically carry out this belief in real-time within your church setting.

If you are still with me, then let me share an opening story with you. I always begin my "Jesus as Pastor" session with this story. The names have not been changed to lay bear the guilty.

Jared Siebert is a good friend of mine and also the Director and Idea Leader of *New Leaf Network*. We have known each other for years. One of my favourite things about being a part of the *Design Shop* teaching team is that I get to hear Jared teach and hang out with him. In my opinion there is no greater expert on issues facing the Evangelical church in Canada today. He also has a great beard and a full head of hair. The former I can compete with; the latter stirs jealousy.

Several years ago Jared and I brought together about 40 church planters. Most were from Southern Ontario but we had participants from across the country. We decided that Jared would begin the time together by introducing a plan for the day, which was to include story sharing, discussion around some missional ideas within the Canadian context, and prayer. It seemed like a perfectly good idea — until Jared began. We had not discussed how he would introduce the day, so what he proceeded to do surprised me. He listed reason after reason why the church in Canada had no hope: It is going to fail. It is failing. Canadian culture is so apathetic to religion that no matter what we do, no one is going care. And in the process of realizing all of this, those of us who are pastors will suffer, sacrifice, and never see any fruit. Jared's tirade and lament started off almost funny, but it soon became a depressing downer and sucked the life and hope right out of the room. Tears fell down Jared's cheeks. He was filled with such despair. Had I have known that this was where his head and heart were at, I may have suggested someone else do the introduction. But then came the moment I will never forget. He paused and stopped. Somehow he managed to look us all in the eye. We were all hanging off the edge of a very depressing cliff. Then he said it. "F*ck it; Jesus wins."[1]

It was powerful and provocative. And I would not have changed any of it. The power and audacity of the word he chose was immediately surpassed by the power and audacity of the follow-up statement: "Jesus wins." It was an instance where the shock value was entirely appropriate and well-placed.

It was in this palpable moment where deep within all of us, despite the obstacles we knew existed, we knew that this simple truth redefined our entire outlook. In fact, in that moment, we could feel the cosmic reality of such a simple statement. No matter the pain, suffering, loss, trials, and lack of victories, we would press on because somehow, in some way, Jesus wins. His church wins. And no matter the challenges, failures and sacrifices, he is with us and for us.

The words Jared spoke hit each of us like a punch to our guts. It was a recognition of a truth that changed everything. My hope is that the following pages leave you with that same feeling. So quit pastoring your church. Instead, let Jesus do it. This idea of Jesus as our pastor is one that can change everything. It has for me.

May it be so for you, too.

---

[1] For those concerned, this is the last time the f-bomb appears in this book. Or any other swearing, for that matter.

The Need for Something Different

1

The Wall

Many a good speaker on the leadership speaking circuit has recognized this truth: that everything rises and falls on leadership. I agree with that assertion. You would have to have been living under a rock for the last 25 years to not notice that this has been a rally cry within Evangelicalism. Authors and speakers have made a living off of this topic and that statement. To an extent, it would seem, I am just another person adding to an already crowded field of commentators. My approach, however, is a little different. While I agree that everything rises and falls on leadership, my question is *whose* leadership? Mine? The title of this book suggests otherwise.

If I am to lead well, then I need to point people to the real leader. If I am to have a church that is infused with the Spirit and power of God, then I need to help shape an environment where God can demonstrate those things. Which means that I am more convinced than ever that leadership matters, but only when Jesus is afforded a place to be the functional leader in our churches. My leadership matters only in so much as I point to Jesus as our church's pastor. It is about me, but not in the way that many of us have been led to believe.

I believe that almost all pastors agree with this — in theory. I cannot imagine anyone suggesting that her or his leadership is more important than the leadership of Jesus. But the functional leadership of Jesus in our ministries must go beyond mere lip service. I believe that allowing Jesus to lead is markedly different than putting a Jesus-slant on secular leadership models. Unfortunately, in my experience and from observation, many traditional leadership models and structures, at best, simply forget that Jesus can and wants to lead us, and at worst, work to remove the functional leadership of Jesus from the equation. A pastor or church can be quite successful if they follow the advice and teachings of the Evangelical leadership machine. They actually do not need Jesus. Many a church has thrived according to many of our Evangelical metrics without involving Jesus at all. But are these churches really living? Are they experiencing the very person of Jesus in their midst?

This is why I start here, with a theology of the pastoral office. We *need* to get this right. We need to quit being all that we have been told we need to be. We need to get out of the way. We need to see ourselves, not as replacements to Jesus' pastoral ministry, but as those who can direct people to it — to show people to Jesus' leadership, not our own.

I do not like to fail. Sometimes when I play sports I hate to lose more than I enjoy to win. There was a day when I was much younger and far less sanctified that my victory celebrations of smiling and raising my arms in the air paled in comparison to my fits of rage upon losing. There are a few broken hockey sticks, helmets, and nets laying around to prove it. For the record, I do not think that this is a noble characteristic.

During one summer of my undergrad degree I, like many brave women and men before me, decided to go tree planting to make large sums of money in a short period of time. If you are unfamiliar with tree planting, allow me to explain. It is not landscaping. It is not gardening. It is hell. If I told you there was a field nearby and that at every metre/yard in straight lines there were dimes sitting on the ground, and all you had to do was walk along picking up dimes all day that you could keep, would you do it? Perhaps. That does not sound too bad. Except then I tell you that until recently there had been a forrest on this field, but the forrest was harvested leaving a landscape of uneven terrain, debris, rocks, holes, and stumps. And some of it will be on a mountainside. *And* there will be millions of black flies each with a personal mission to drive you insane, so much so that although it is incredibly hot and humid outside, you will need to wear a black coloured bug screen over your head to keep them off of you. And then when the sun goes behind a cloud and you experience life-giving reprieve from its hot rays, mosquitos the size of bumblebees will attack you as if you are the last source of hot blood on earth. Oh, and do not forget the bears. Yes, bears. Bears that might eat you.

And you will pick up these dimes, stuck in the debris of trees and rock, from sun up to sun down, stopping only to eat the lunch you packed yourself in the morning, which was the last time you saw a human being before you were dropped in the middle of nowhere to pick up those stupid dimes.

That is tree planting. Except replace the picking up dimes with slamming your shovel into the ground and planting a 10-inch tree every metre/yard that you carry around by the hundred in a bag hanging off your waste. Yes, the money can be great, but the job is beyond terrible. *That* is tree planting.

Well I did it. Sort of.

I remember one of the first weeks I was out "on the block," as we called it. One of the tree planting veterans told me, a rookie, about "the wall." He spoke about it like he was a great-grandpa telling his great-grandchild about a battle in which he fought during a great war. He told me about "the wall" like it was living thing which he had encountered but could barely bring himself to talk about aloud.

"Aaron, one day you will be out there planting, and you are going to feel like you know what you are doing. You are going to start believing you can do it; that you can be the greatest tree planter ever. And then you will come across it. You will not see it coming, but when you come to it you will wonder how you never saw it in the distance. Because it is huge. It spans as far as you can see in both directions and as high as the sky. You will not get around it. It will stop you where you stand. It will laugh at you. You will try to keep going, but let me give you some advice: embrace 'the wall.' Do not fight it. Do not get angry. Just admit you cannot do it. Sit down. Give up. And wait."

I thought the description sounded a tad dramatic. But then I learned it may not have been dramatic enough. It was midday with the sun beating down on me. I had put about 125 trees in the ground and was starting to feel like I might hit my goal for the day: 200 trees which equaled a $200 payday. Then I ran into a section of earth where beneath about two inches of soil there was rock. Everywhere, rock. Every time I slammed the blade of my shovel into the ground to create the 6-8 inch slot needed to slide the little tree root into, my blade rung off the rock like a tuning fork. Pain would shoot up my arm and my whole body would shake as I questioned the goodness of God in creating this stupid rock. (Your mind goes to a lot of dark places while you tree plant.) Flies ate me. They took my blood and seemed to bite me for the fun of it. It was at least 30 degrees celsius and it was unbearably humid. I was sweating to the point it looked liked I had just stepped out of a shower, only to then stop sweating completely after all of my water reserves had emptied. And to make matters worse, that morning on the way to the area in which I would be planting, I had stepped in a huge hole filled with disgusting swamp water that had flooded one of my boots and soaked my sock and foot (growing up in Manitoba we called these "booters"). The dampness in my boot was creating a rubbing effect that was now making me think I would be better off without that foot.

After 30 minutes of walking around in this state, slamming my shovel into rock and not making a cent, it appeared. The wall. It grimaced at me like some crazed animal from a horror movie. I paced to the right and to the left looking for a way around it. But no luck. I could not get around. I was done. The wall had won. I threw my shovel to the ground, took off the bag of trees weighing me down, and collapsed. The eery description the veteran planter had given me came rushing to my mind. He was right. There was nothing I could do but sit there and wait. It dawned on me then that I did not know what I was waiting for. Then it hit me. It was a moment of decision. Will I get up and keep going, or will I quit?

I am proud to say that I stood up, picked up my shovel, and quit. Yes, I was a quitter. Okay, so this is not the story I will tell my kids someday to encourage them to keep going when life gets tough. This will be the story I tell them when they need to know that sometimes life kicks your butt. Within days of this terrible event I was on my way home, tail between my legs, admitting defeat at the hands of the evil wall.

The point of sharing this flattering story with you is simply to point out what we all know and would confess if we had the guts to be honest and vulnerable with each other: we have all hit the proverbial wall at least once in our life. Likely the circumstances vary, for sure, but we all know about the wall. It is encountered in those moments when we come to the end of ourselves, our own strength, our own capacity to keep going, and we realize that something must change because the status quo no longer works.

Maybe the way we best grasp new paradigms and make substantial changes in our life happens when we realize the failure of beliefs or practices to which we previously clung. The wall might be terrible or painful, but it demands change that can sometimes be life-giving. I thought I could be a good tree planter. I had planned to make lots of money. In this case, my new paradigm and the substantial change prompted me to quit and return home; I soon found a job driving an air-conditioned tractor all day making the same amount of money. It turned out okay. But there are far more serious and substantive shifts we make in our life.

After a decade in full-time ministry as a youth pastor in an established traditional Evangelical church, and working on higher education, I ventured out on my own as a church planter. It could be assumed that one's personal faults and misconceptions about ministry when you are an assistant pastor are less visible than in solo leadership. Whether or not that is true, for me, moving into a solo ministry was a recipe for a huge personal shake-up. I quickly realized that I would not be able to get the job done unless something changed. It was another wall moment, but this time a far more serious one than a frustrating summer job.

I moved to Ancaster, ON, believing some pretty ridiculous things about myself and what I was going to accomplish as a church planter. Ancaster is a white-collar town. It is home to educated, high-capacity people. Doctors, lawyers, professors, teachers, CEOs, CFOs, entrepreneurs, business owners: these are the types of people who live in Ancaster. I was convinced that we — that *I* — was going to do church in such a sophisticated, intellectual, and clever way, that people would be flocking to be baptized. I would preach in ways that would put hearts on fire for Jesus. This particular demographic of people would be amazed at the intellectual integrity of my faith. I fancied myself a smart guy for smart people.

My fingers tremble writing this. How ridiculous. How arrogant. How misguided. How wrong I was.

It was over coffee with my friend, mentor, and key leader in our new church, Dr. Lee Beach,[1] that I hit the wall, or that I at least recognized it was right there in front of me. We were talking about the future of our infant church, the potential we had to see people come to faith, the possibility of Christians joining us in this new expression of the church —you know, all the sorts of things you talk about when you are in the first months of a new church — and the wall appeared, fast, strong, and enormous. It was one of those times when you hear yourself say something and it dawns on you that it will never work. I was talking about the future of our church — this great potential I saw in it and myself — and I suddenly realized that if this church's future hinged on me, we were not going to make it. The task was overwhelming. My inability to make it happen was staring me in the face. I felt we were doomed.

Tears began to fall down my cheeks. I broke. In that little coffee shop I came to realize that unless Jesus "showed up" and did

---

[1] Lee is Associate Professor of Christian Ministry, Garbutt F. Smith Chair of Ministry Formation, and Director of Ministry Formation at *McMaster Divinity College* in Hamilton, Ontario, Canada.

his thing, we did not stand a chance. I could not do it alone. I could not bring to the table enough wow-factor to make it work. Nothing we were going to do was going to make people flock to us asking to be baptized and wondering where they could start tithing. I could not preach well enough to draw crowds. I was not a celebrity and very likely never would be. Despite our sincere intentions to serve and love our community, that likely would not be enough to make the Kingdom explode in the streets. I had an intense revelation that we needed Jesus. Like, we needed the real Jesus in the flesh. We needed him to walk into the room and do his thing. We needed Jesus to lead us, to speak to us, to do signs and wonders, to speak through us, and to use us. If we did not create an environment in which he could be the show, so to speak, this little church was never going to be faithful to what God was putting before us. The vision, the dream, the desires: none of it would happen if we did not have the real presence of Jesus leading us. But I only sort-of believed he could show up. I only sort-of believed he even wanted to do those things. And then another frightening thought entered my mind: If he cannot or does not do those things, it is over. None of what I had to offer would be enough to sustain long-term ministry or help to shape a fruitful church. If my early journey as a church planter had taught me anything, it was that despite the leadership training I had received from the Evangelical machine, I was in great need. I was not enough.

I have been a Christian for decades. I celebrate Easter. I believe Jesus died and rose again. I believe that through the power of the Spirit, Jesus speaks even today. I believe he can do signs and wonders. But what I realized in that moment in the coffee shop was that I did not *functionally* believe those things. I believed them on paper — even in my heart — but I did not believe them in real life. The fact is, until that point I had not needed to believe them. Until that moment I believed that my skills as a leader could carry me well enough. I had been taught about leadership. I had the principals down pretty good. But on that day, up against the wall, I came to the end of that belief. And I was terrified. I realized for the first time that I needed Jesus. I needed *him*— not just the idea of him, but him. I needed his voice. I needed his healing. I needed his leadership. And I became convinced that if our church had any sort of positive future, it needed him just as much and in all the same ways. It is an expression you have likely heard before, but it became real for me in those days: I did not want to talk about Jesus like he was not in the room. I wanted him in the room. I wanted to feel his presence. I wanted to hear his voice.

I wish I could say that from that moment on, things turned around, that my epiphany that day started me on a beautiful road toward healing and joy. Not so. Things just got worse. (More to come on that later.) However, one train of thought began to develop. As I hit the wall I began to wrestle with my title and job description. The wrestling was about the theology behind those things. What is a pastor of a local church? What is my baseline understanding of what I do and represent? And just as pressing, what am I not? Hitting the wall that day made me question what, intentionally or *not*, I had come to believe about leadership within the Evangelical world.

As a church planter I found myself answering a certain set of questions quite often: "Where does your church meet?", "What does your service look like?", "How many people are in your group?", "What is your church's name?" and "What is your role?" were typical. Because of the frequency of these questions, most of my answers became concise and at the ready. Some questions were easy to answer. But my answer to the "What is your role?" question was always a tricky one. And after hitting the wall in the coffee shop it became even more difficult to articulate. However, what began in that moment was an exciting job identity crisis.

There are many potential roles a pastor takes on, both within the context of church and extending out into the community. As a start, the standard roles in which most pastors engage include: counsellor, prophet, gate-keeper, theology teacher, deliverer of religious goods and services (e.g., we marry, bury, and sign official documents), leader, consensus-builder, mediator, shepherd, encourager, evangelist, apostle, servant, administrator, and vision-caster. As a pastor of a *church plant*, you also perform janitorial duties, such as fixing toilets and emptying garbages, you lift heavy objects, and even wash toys. However, I would suggest that above all else, the pastor of a church functions as a public test-case. That while a pastor's engagements may include all or some of those roles listed above, ultimately he or she functions as the most public demonstration of the redeeming work of Christ. I believe that the pastor and laity are equal in terms of value, but that the pastor is distinct in their personal exposure to public scrutiny and observation. In real terms, it means we get to show everyone how broken, full of doubt, and messed up we are. We get to stand at the front and be an example of how much humanity needs Jesus. Our public willingness to authentically show our need for Jesus' presence in our life is a privilege, albeit a painful one. Oddly enough I have never seen that description listed in a pastoral job posting, but this new awareness became my base theology moving forward.

Here's Paul in 1 Corinthians 4...

> *I suppose that God has shown that we apostles are at the end of the line. We are like prisoners sentenced to death, because we have become a spectacle in the world, both to angels and to humans. We are fools for Christ, but you are wise through Christ! We are weak, but you are strong! You are honoured, but we are dishonoured! Up to this very moment we are hungry, thirsty, wearing rags, abused, and homeless. We work hard with our own hands. When we are insulted, we respond with a blessing; when we are harassed, we put up with it; when our reputation is attacked, we are encouraging. We have become the scum of the earth, the waste that runs off everything, up to the present time.*

1 Corinthians 4:9-13

When is the last time you heard this text read at an ordination or pastor's induction service? It is not a passage that makes for good celebrations, balloons, cake, and after-service parties. And I cannot recall hearing any pastor mention this passage in his or her calling story.

As Paul describes himself, he suggests that in his role as pastor, he has been made a spectacle to provocatively illustrate the kingdom. Spectacle can be understood as theatre. Essentially, Paul claims that he is an actor on a stage for all to see. With his famous sarcasm he lambastes the Corinthians for misunderstanding the way to true life. The way is not through the means they assumed: glory, honour, and strength. Rather, the way to life is through death and utter dependency on Jesus. Paul accepted the role of being the most public demonstration of weakness and death-to-self so that those around him would not see him, but rather, the glory of the Saviour. Paul's experiences evoke the reality of Jesus' life: it is through weakness and death that life is found and demonstrated.

The Corinthians did not admire that Jesus was crucified on a Roman cross. From their perspective, a Saviour would not die that kind of dishonourable death. And the Corinthians did not think much of Paul as a guy who worked "with his hands." High-profile honourable (i.e., celebrity) leaders then or now do not get their hands dirty. The Corinthians just did not get it.

One of my favourite professors in seminary, Dr. Michael Knowles,[2] said it best: "Pastors ought to be a demonstration of the failure of the human project." Pastors ought to demonstrate that we do not trade our life for Jesus' life when we are saved. No, we exchange our life for Jesus' *death*, and it is through that process that we find life.

---

2 Michael is Professor of Preaching and the George F. Hurlburt Chair of Preaching at *McMaster Divinity College* in Hamilton, Ontario, Canada.

Did you catch that? This is perhaps the most overlooked aspect of becoming a follower of Jesus. We exchange life for death to find life. This is not the glamourous call to salvation we too often try to sell. The mysterious life of salvation is one of death and life, over and over again.

Therefore as pastors, we become "the scum of the earth, the waste that runs off everything," so that we might decrease and Jesus might increase. And no one does this more publicly in the church than the pastor. Our congregations ought to see us frequently processing our own death. We are a test-case for the impossibility of the human project; we prove that we cannot fix ourselves and we certainly cannot be the superstar that we sometimes so badly want to be. We have the privilege, and the unfortunate pleasure, of demonstrating that Christ in me is the only hope of glory. This is my role. I am, and must continually be, the most public demonstration in my church of someone who cannot live apart from Jesus. Certainly, every Christian ought to work from the same foundational belief, but not every Christian gets to have the whole church watch while it is happening. If you are reading this and wondering about becoming a pastor, this is the point where you think twice. I *love* my job. But there is a vulnerability I experience that is both exciting and terrifying. You cannot fake this job and live at peace. You cannot call people to transformation and God's grace and mercy while not having a testimony of those things. You have to smoke what you are selling, or people will see right through you. More critically, they will not likely see Jesus.

It is worth noting that throughout Paul's ministry, whenever he talks about his pastoral vocation, he does not usually talk about himself as a transmitter of God's mercy and hope, but instead a recipient of God's mercy and hope. Grace and mercy were not Paul's to offer. There is something incredibly profound here. There is one mediator and his name is Jesus. What I see and have experienced in Jesus — what I hear and touch — is what I have received and can then share. In other words, I am a storyteller. I can point people to the one who the story is about. I can talk about how Jesus' story has shaped mine and invite people into the same experience. As a pastor, regardless of the words I speak, people will watch me and see my story. My story will either demonstrate my own power(lessness), or it will demonstrate his.

I wish I could say that I came to this conclusion over night and have been living it out flawlessly ever since. That is certainly not the case. The experience with the wall lasted for months, and in many ways it continues to this day. Yet in those days to follow the coffeeshop discussion with Lee, I began to revisit how we needed to shape and change things in our church, even in its young age. We would need to discern new models for pointing to Jesus as the pastor. I would need to change my own thinking on what leadership looked like for me and help others to change their expectations of me and of Jesus. These tasks prompted me to consider an extremely basic yet profound question I had to ask myself and our church:

did we believe Jesus was alive?

2

Do We Believe Jesus Is Alive, Can Speak, & Lead?

My daughter, who is in elementary school, came home upset not too long ago. We were planning a party to celebrate her birthday and she had asked several friends to join us. One said no. Understandably, my daughter felt rejected and hurt. Why would the friend not come? My wife Shalene knew the answer. She informed us that this girl was a part of a family that practices the faith of Jehovah's Witnesses. Case solved. They do not celebrate or attend birthday parties. When we said this to my daughter she quickly responded with the obvious question: "Why?" Without missing a beat I began to respond, but as the words started coming out of my mouth I stopped myself. It was one of those moments when you hear yourself saying words that prompt you to realize something does not add up. Try not to judge me too much, but I was about to respond by saying, "Because they believe some crazy things." However, as soon as I began to say, "They believe some cr...", I had to stop. Wait a second; I believe some crazy things, do I not? Before I go mocking other religions for having "crazy" beliefs, I ought to look in the mirror. Although my response was going to be delivered somewhat tongue-in-cheek, I could not go through with it because I was immediately convicted that I am supposed to believe some pretty wild things, too.

Truth be told, I do find it hard. It is hard to embrace the Christian story. I believe in a guy that was born of a virgin some 2000 years ago, lived the life of a nomadic healer and prophet, was killed on a cross, came back to life three days later, and is now somewhere alive and well in human form and, through the mystery of the Holy Spirit, is able to be mystically present among us today. Um, that sounds a little crazy to me. But that *is* what we believe as Christians. And we do not just believe it, we participate in it, embedded in the story, or at least we are invited to do so. In fact, the entire hope of the Christian faith is bound to these crazy facts. Unfortunately for my daughter, my response then turned into a ten minute nuanced explanation of world religions, practices, and beliefs. I think I lost her after a few seconds, but I am sure that when she is older she will thank me.

The thing is, so many of us believe in the living Christ, but are functional cessationists. We balk at our own beliefs. Sure, we all have doubts. Doubting is essential to life and certainly has its place, but when it cripples a pastor to the point of paralysis, it can be devastating. As pastors we can lead giving lip service to the leadership and presence of Jesus, but our day-to-day structures and leadership culture often remove his real-time presence. Often even intentionally. We refer to Jesus as healer, but are terrified to invite him into the room as the great physician. We preach sermons about listening to his voice, but rarely wait with openness to hear him speak or to ask what others are hearing from him. We can talk a lot about discernment, but the processes we use for such an activity tend to lean more towards keeping order and ensuring majority rules than inviting and listening to the voice of the Spirit. The actions we would expect from a friend who is physically in the room with us are not what we expect from Jesus. Instead, we lead, create structures, vote on issues, pray, shape policies, put our best business strategies in play — all without ever asking if the guy in the corner, Jesus, has anything to say on the matter. We can talk about him like he is in the room, but then never invite him into the circle to participate.

Do we believe Jesus is alive and present? Can we embrace our craziness? Can we lead in such a way that directs people to an active, living, Jesus? His presence is essential. I dare to say that without it we are not actually practicing Christians because we have ignored the core essence of our faith.

Call it cheesy if you like, but in our church gatherings we always begin by lighting a candle. This is not creative or groundbreaking; our more liturgical cousins in the faith have been doing this sort of thing for centuries. That candle, though, draws our attention: it is the focal point. Beside the candle is an icon of "Christ the light-giver." It is a Byzantine image of Jesus holding open the Scripture passage from John 8:12. I do not for a moment imagine that this image of Jesus is an accurate portrayal of his likeness, but that is not the point in its intentional placement. In front of the candle is the bread and wine in which we partake each week. Flanking those items is a jar of oil for anointing, a small Roman Catholic-styled crucifix[1], a small Armenian Orthodox cross[2], and the Bible.

All of these objects on a table are front and centre, not the band, the screen, or the preacher. These iconic elements remind us of someone's presence with us: Jesus.

We do not worship those images, but they correct our gaze; they are a representation of where Jesus sits in our presence as he joins us in the weekly gathering. With great joy and a smile, I have watched over the years as people point to this table when they are referring to Jesus being with us. It is like they are pointing at and referring to any other real person who is present with us on that Sunday. "You know Jesus, he sits right over here with us." This simple visual portrayal is one of the aspects of our little group that I have grown to love dearly. We are the crazy people

---

1 The image of Jesus crucified on the cross.
2 The image of Jesus resurrected and no longer on the cross.

that talk about Jesus while he sits amongst us.

The presence of Jesus must be the distinguishing factor in our churches. Good, bad, or ugly, every church is known for something. "They are the big church with great music." "They are the church that does missions really well." "They are the church that serves the community." All of that is lovely, but imagine hearing about the church where Jesus is present — where the stories that come out of a church community are about the presence of Jesus being so palpable that you would think he was there in the flesh walking around. Some churches are distinctive in this way, and it is captivating, exhilarating, life-giving, and exciting.

To be sure, I am not intending to create a false-dichotomy. You could argue that being known for serving the community or being great at missions does demonstrate the presence of Jesus. And it may be that being known for those things help people move to a place in their lives where they could meet Jesus. Absolutely. But I have been a part of churches that do great things and yet never did I participate in anything that would lead me to believe that a local non-religious charity group could not have done the same thing. What sets Christian churches apart from local service clubs? What sets us apart from the well-run organization in town that cares for people because that is just what good people do? Our distinguishing factor is this: we do all of these great things — in partnership with Jesus — to share his presence with people and to communally share in his presence. If we do not invite him into the room, if we do not teach people to hear him, if we do not give him functional leadership in our church, we will too often help to shape nice people but not people who have been transformed by his living voice, power, and presence. And there is a difference, which must be laid bare. A nice person may not know how to deal with brokenness, sin and depravity. A nice person may not fully grasp the beauty of the universal timeless re-creation of the universe under God's good guidance. A nice person may not ever distinguish the voice of the one who is in all, through all, and giving life to all. *Jesus* is what sets us apart. If he is only there in lip service, we miss out. There is a difference between nice people and those who have tasted and seen that the Lord is good.

The view of the early church throughout the New Testament is that Jesus continued to minister after his ascension. He was gone, but he was present. This seeming paradox elicits, for many of us, doubt. I find myself relating over and over again to the conversation between Doubting Thomas and Jesus. Thomas needed to see the physical Jesus to believe, and was blessed to be with Jesus. He was one of the lucky few. But then Jesus says something that sometimes gives me encouragement and other times prompts me to cry out, "But how?"

> *Jesus replied [to Thomas], "Do you believe because you see me? Happy are those who don't see and yet believe."*
>
> John 20:29

One of the most painful and yet liberating experiences of my life happened because of this verse.

I mentioned before that life continued to get worse and fall apart soon after my coffee shop chat with Lee. Within weeks of that experience my world turned upside down. The wall took on a whole new meaning. Everything I once believed to be in control spiralled chaotically. My wife received a cancer diagnosis of melanoma. My eldest son began having seizures. And the Canadian Revenue Agency sent me a letter claiming I owed them $25,000. All within two weeks of the coffeeshop chat.

As you might imagine, I did not react well. I fell apart. Most days were spent sitting on my couch in my pajamas, unable to do anything beyond pouring through Scripture searching for anything to give me hope. Sometimes I found glimpses. Sometimes it just made my family's circumstances more confusing and hard to understand. I was in really rough shape. I doubted everything: my faith, if Jesus was real, if anything on which I had based my life was true. It was a faith identity crisis, to say the least. I was mentally wrecked to the point of it manifesting in all sorts of bizarre physical ways. If you have experienced extreme anxiety before then you know how this looks. Intense anxiety soon shifts to severe depression which leads to numbness. My body and mind felt as though it had been chased by a ravenous tiger, and it soon just shut down. To call this time of my life a "dark valley" just does not cut it. I could not function. It was bad. And through it all, my faith allegiance was completely up for grabs. I recall a few times when the pull between dark and light felt so strong that I literally said aloud to Satan or whatever evil was listening, "No!"

On one particular day I was reading through the Gospel of John. I came to chapter 20 and I had to stop reading immediately following verse 28.

> *Thomas, the one called Didymus, one of the Twelve, wasn't with the disciples when Jesus came. The other disciples told him, "We've seen the Lord!" But he replied, "Unless I see the nail marks in his hands, put my finger in the wounds left by the nails, and put my hand into his side, I won't believe."*
>
> *After eight days his disciples were again in a house and Thomas was with them. Even though the doors were locked, Jesus entered and stood among them. He said, "Peace be with you." Then he said to Thomas, "Put your finger here. Look at my hands. Put your hand into my side. No more disbelief. Believe!" Thomas responded to Jesus, "My Lord and my God!"*

John 20:24-28

I put down my Bible. It was a full brake, emergency stop, grinding halt. With my faith in question, my loyalty to this thing called Christianity incredibly thin, and a desire for *anything* to give me hope, I closed my tear-filled eyes, and I asked Jesus for the same privilege. I promised that I would not open my eyes. I just needed to touch him. I needed to know he was real. I had serious doubts. I was no longer sure if any of this was real. I was ready to give it all up and walk away — forget the church plant, forget all of it. I needed to touch him; I needed proof. And as I sat there, tears streaming down my face, with my eyes sealed and my arm and hand literally outstretched and shaking, ready to touch the Son of God, nothing happened. I felt nothing. I gave it a good minute. Eyes closed and pleading for something.

But nothing.

In despair and utter disappointment, I reopened my Bible and kept reading into verse 29. I am not sure why, but when I put my Bible down after reading verse 28 I did not remember what happened next in the story.

> *Jesus replied, "Do you believe because you see me? Happy are those who don't see and yet believe."*
>
> John 20:29

It was as if the line was delivered from the lips of Jesus himself right into my ears. Ten seconds earlier I was filled with despair, and then I heard him speak. The words came off the page like he was sitting with me and saying them to me. It was a moment of presence that felt just as real as if I had actually touched him. It was incredible.

All of my problems, doubts, and fears were certainly not solved in that moment, but a rush of Jesus' love and encouragement filled my spirit. For that day, at least, it was what I needed to keep going. I did not touch him that day, yet I did. And so it is with so many things in this journey called the Christian faith: inextricable moments of both absence and presence. Moments that we cannot explain with scientific analysis, but that we cannot deny.

Moments that ask us to embrace our own "crazy." Jesus is alive. He is present. I will cry out and I will wait with expectation for his response.

The stories of our ancestors of the faith certainly point to the trustworthiness of these statements. Others before us have walked this journey. The overwhelming evidence of Scripture is that when we are in need, God is present. Far more often than not, God responds to those who enquire of him. God speaks. The window into our forebears' prayer lives in the Psalms reminds us that as confident as they were that God would hear them, they were equally expectant in his ability and willingness to reply. They rested in this two-fold experience.

> *I cry out loud to the Lord, and he answers me from his holy mountain.*
>
> Psalm 3:4

> *LORD, in the morning you hear my voice. In the morning I lay it all out before you. Then I wait expectantly.*
>
> Psalm 5:3

It was during these darkest of days that meat was being put on the bones of my faith. I was learning so much about listening prayer and intentionally asking Jesus to reveal what he was doing around me. Again, these were all practices I mostly believed on paper and in my heart before this time, but I had never practiced them. In God's good providence he surrounded me with people during this time who helped strengthen my capacity in these practices. One exercise I was encouraged to begin was simply asking Jesus to show me where he was in the midst of darkness. On paper, we believe he is never absent, but in reality we feel like he often is. The question "Where were you?" is so very important because I have learned that he often desperately wants to share with us the answer.

One day I asked Jesus to reveal to me where he was on the day of my wife's cancer diagnosis. I have never felt such absence of goodness than I did on that day. I sat on my couch with my eyes closed and asked him, the circumstances of the experience playing back like a movie in my mind.

We had had a couple of friends visiting us from out of town, and as I was just getting ready to carry their suitcases out to the car to make our way to the airport when the phone rang. It was the call from the doctor which revealed the test results: she had cancer. My wife broke down immediately, but instead of being able to hold her I had to get our friends to the airport. The timing was not ideal. The drive to and from the airport felt like days. I was just trying to keep my eyes on the road and get home to Shalene.

When I returned and walked back into our house I immediately found her crumpled up in the fetal position on our kitchen floor, crying and scared. I was paralyzed; I couldn't move. I just stood there looking at her. Our young kids were upstairs playing, completely unaware of what was happening. It was at this exact moment that Jesus focused my attention. He said, "Aaron, where do you see me?" As I relived that moment in my mind I looked for Jesus. I saw him sitting on the kitchen floor, holding Shalene. Her tears were falling on his arm. He held her with ultimate compassion and tenderness. I knew as I was watching this unfold that he was telling me that through all of the upcoming journey, he was going to teach her about love — his incredible love for her. He held her, not explaining why it was happening, but what was going to happen now. She was going to encounter the Father's love in a way she never had before.

Then it was my turn. I looked for Jesus near me. And there he was. He stood in front of me like a teacher at the front of classroom. I felt as if I was in one of those old-school desks where the seat is connected to the table. I was sitting and he was in front of me teaching. He was going to teach me how to hear him, to see him, and to know him in a way I had never thought possible. I was going to learn that Jesus is real, that he is *for* me, and that I can expect his presence.

This whole visual experience was the first time I had experienced such a powerful image of Jesus with me, but it would not be the last.

My theology is such that I do not believe God caused the cancer, the seizures, or any of the difficult circumstances. But without doubt he is the great teacher and he will always insert himself to breathe into our lives redemption and new beginnings. He will make beauty appear; it is what he does. I was beginning to come to terms with my Christian craziness because I experienced the presence of Jesus in a way I never had before. Apparently, he is alive.

For many of us this is not easy: believing we can hear a voice from someone who is in the room but is not in the room. Can we live with an expectation that Jesus is present, though we cannot see him? Can we expect his voice, his signs, his wonders, his touch, and his desire to lead us? Can we ask him to reveal himself and expect that he will? This is the stuff that cannot be explained to doubters; it is the stuff that makes us look and sound crazy. But I am confident that it is the essential distinguishing factor for us as the Christian church: our crazy belief in the presence of a living Jesus.

I am becoming increasingly comfortable with my own craziness.

How to Try
Something Different

3

Who Are Your Prophets?

Allow me to make a bold claim to get the ball rolling: too many processes and practices in the church work to remove the functional leadership of Jesus. Yes, you read that correctly. I believe we often *intentionally* act to remove the presence of Jesus as our leader. Something inside of us tells us that inviting Jesus into the process is too risky. Why do we think this? We might articulate our fears in various ways: fear of our own belief in the craziness we have discussed, how we might look, fear of getting it wrong, fear of change, fear of abuse of power, or fear of a faith that seems too charismatic. But we must embrace our fear, not as a reason to stop moving forwards, but rather as an indication that good questions and potential wisdom are evident in what we seek. Fear can also give us a window into our faith and into some of the things that we need to be vulnerable with to both God and to our church.

Many questions and thoughts, rooted in fear, immediately present themselves: What if we intentionally create space for God to speak and we try to listen, but nothing happens when we invite Jesus into the process? What if we create too much expectation for God's power and presence, and people's expectations are not met? What if my own expectations are not met? After all, I am supposed to lead this; it could be disastrous if I lose faith. I could have some explaining to do if the results do not equal the hype. I could inadvertently drive people further away from Jesus by messing this all up! What if it is just me manufacturing a feeling or a voice in my head? Certainly these are all legitimate, real concerns. Inviting the functional leadership of Jesus into our churches can seem scary. And as mentioned, we absolutely need to use wisdom. I wonder, though, if for many leaders, as it was in me, there lay seeded a disbelief that God is *for* us. I sometimes doubt that in Christ, God is victorious; that Jesus, despite his ascension, is still with us and for us. If I could be convinced that God is for me and nothing can stand against me, would I be more interested in being a fool for him? Would I then take the risk of opening up the floor to him?

In the middle of John's Gospel we are drawn into the heart of Jesus for his followers and the future of the church. He expresses his desire for companionship and partnership in mission, and sets out to remind those listening that no matter what fear stands before them, he is not going anywhere, he has won and will continue to win, and he will work in pursuit to bring his followers alongside him. Like a seasoned veteran who is calling on the rookies to follow him because he has been there before, felt what they feel, and because he will show them the way and take care of them, Jesus reminds his followers in John 15 and 16 that they are on the winning team. He will not abandon them. Even after his ascension, Jesus claims, he will send *the Companion* to be just that: a companion in the journey, leading his followers into truth.

> *He will guide you in all truth. He won't speak on his own, but will say whatever he hears and will proclaim to you what is to come.*

> John 16:13

Jesus is building a solid case for why following him into this sort of real-time experience is worth it: "In case you are still nervous about this whole idea, do not worry, I am coming back and, by the way, I have conquered the world" (John 16:33), "I am going to pray for you who follow me and your friends who do not yet know me" (John 17:9, 20), and "I am going to be *in* you" (John 17:26). Talk about encouragement!

If we are willing to dive into those statements and risk that they just might be true, then we can start on this exciting journey of shaping new, or adjusting old, systems that have worked to hold these statements at arm's length. Jesus is for us and he wants us to get this right. He wants to let us into the triune conversation taking place. He wants us to partner with him in what he is doing. It is *his* church and its success rides on *his* shoulders. He is asking us to believe him at his word; he will accomplish what he began, and you are invited to join him in the process.

So where do we start? In this chapter I will begin by asking the questions do you know who the prophets are in your church? And are they involved in your decision-making processes and day-to-day life as a church? Then in the next chapter I'll ask if your church's decision-making processes involve Jesus? Do they involve worship, quiet, study of Scriptures, contemplation, prayer, and intentional times of listening to the voice of Jesus? My hope is that these questions will get you started in assessing how your current processes and environments may or may not be inviting Jesus to lead and presence himself.

Prophets.

The image of a man or woman pointing a finger while yelling, "Thus sayeth the Lord" may be one of the reasons why this first question puts you in a defensive posture. We have all seen people abuse the title "prophet" in a way that prompts feelings of weariness or suspicion in our spirit. If your experience of a prophet is someone who makes you feel bad, worthless, guilty or full of shame, then I want to suggest you have not actually experienced or encountered a prophet. Or at least not a very good one. These are not the sort of prophets I am talking about.

I confess that the title and office of prophet was among the things I believed on paper, but had very little practical use for in my early ministry days. The closest thing to a prophet I had ever experienced was U2's Bono, and I am certain the only reason I thought that was because I had read it in some artsy Christian hipster book (not that it was wrong). If I came across someone who I sensed had a prophetic leaning, I immediately thought that either I or that person were in the wrong church. We did not belong together. I attended or served in the non-crazy church. Prophets belonged at the local charismatic church.

When my church planting journey began I met two women. One I met because of a denominational partnership between our new church and an established church on the other side of the country which she attended. Even from a distance, Joanne quickly became invested in our church's life. Because of the partnership between the churches she even had the opportunity to visit us on a sort-of "missions trip." The majority of the time, though, our correspondence was through email. The other woman, Alison, heard about our upstart church and she and her family joined us in the early days, quickly becoming part of our core group. Both of these women have taught me so much about the prophetic gifting and office. Without hesitation I see them as prophets, and I cannot imagine my journey, or our church's journey, without them.

Walter Brueggemann's book, *Prophetic Imagination*, is a good starting place for explaining the giftings of both Joanne and Alison.[1] Brueggemann uses the prophetic examples of the Old Testament to point out that one of the primary roles of the prophet is to, first, point out or acknowledge that which is broken in a situation, and second, to breathe into life an image, idea, or discussion that points to a new and better reality. A prophet opens up a

---
[1] Ausburg Fortress, 2001.

window to imagine a scenario or circumstance that is better, new, and ultimately reflective of God's preferred outcome on earth. If there is a need to offer challenge or rebuke, a prophet will do this. But the rebuke is never the end goal. There is always a better way — God's way. The prophet helps others to imagine a better way forward. How do they do this? How do they know the better way? Because they have seen it, felt it, and heard it. They have a peculiar, divine, and mysterious view into the heart of God. They dwell there intentionally for long periods of time. They nurture it. They tend to it. God affords them the ability to see that which, for all sorts of reasons, many of us cannot. I am sure that one of the primary explanations for this particular gifting is that prophets invest time in a way that escapes most of us. And although what they share with others can sometimes be predictive in nature, I have noticed that it usually is not. They usually share an image, a feeling, a sense. Their sense is not exact direction, but it is always informative, transformational, encouraging, and prompts new beginnings. And it is always, always, presented in humility. Sternness or anger, rarely expressed, is only ever rooted in deep pain and righteous anguish; sentiments are tenderly shared and are never out of spite or arrogance. Words are humbly submitted, never held over someone. My experience has been that when a word is given that is somewhat harsh, it is usually accompanied by fear and trembling and many tears. There is no finger pointing. There is usually a cup of coffee.

There is much about the giftings that Alison and Joanne share for which I am envious. But their gifts also come with a great personal burden which they each must bear. Imagine seeing and feeling what pains the heart of God, and sensing what it is that must be done to move a person towards redemption, only to often have your words and longings fall on deaf ears — to rarely see change quick enough to satisfy that longing. To see glimpses of what could be, only to live in the reality of brokenness: it is a weight I cannot fathom. I see that for my prophet friends this can be exhausting, frustrating, and demoralizing. They require encouragement and support to sustain their difficult calling. But make no mistake, they are a gift. They are more than a gift, in fact; they are a necessary component to the life of the church. We need them. I need them.

The middle section of 1 Corinthians is a masterpiece of writing concerning the functions and mystical unity of the local church. Worship, gifts, communion: it is all there. In chapter 12, after commenting on the beauty, power, and reality of the spiritual gifts, which all believers are given, Paul moves into his famous metaphor of the body. Obviously the gift of prophecy is one of those parts, no more important than others, but like the rest, necessary. However, what is particularly interesting to this discussion is what comes next:

> *And God has appointed in the church first apostles, second prophets, third teachers; then deeds of power, then gifts of healing, forms of assistance, forms of leadership, various kinds of tongues.*
>
> 1 Cor 12:28, NRSV

Unfortunately verse 28 is sometimes read as a statement of hierarchy: that apostles are the most important, followed by prophets and down the list we go. But clearly this cannot be Paul's intention considering what he wrote preceding this statement in his use of the body metaphor. Rather, I believe this statement describes how local churches are created. I believe this is a church planting verse. Someone — an apostle — will instigate the gathering of people in order to become a church. That is not to say there cannot be others already interested in becoming a church, but somebody, at some point, says, "Let's do this." That person is led by the Spirit in one way or another to take the lead in a particular context. I am quite comfortable calling that person an apostle.

Next comes the prophet. I never saw the value in this role before I witnessed it. God's order of creation for the local church to become a church and function as a church in a local community has the gift of prophecy right at the beginning. Following an apostle, you need a prophet: someone who has their heart tuned into the heart of God the way only a prophet can. You need someone who can see and sense brokenness and help everyone around them to imagine a better way. Alison and Joanne became our prophets. They still are.

In the dark months following my wall experience in the coffee shop, when Shalene and I were barely making it through each day, we leaned on Alison and Joanne, night after night. We needed Jesus. We needed his voice. We needed to know he was seeing what was going on with us and that he was not going to abandon us. We always heard Jesus when we spent time with these two women. Joanne sent emails each day from across the country, essentially letting us in on her prayers for us, our circumstances, our kids, our health, our church — everything. Shalene and I would lay in bed next to each other, listening as one of us read the email aloud. The words fell on us like Jesus was in the room speaking them over us like a gentle rain. We would cry, laugh, and find strength to keep going. It was Joanne's writing but Jesus' words. The words always pointed us to God's good truth, his good presence, and his good promises. The words reshaped our context, moulded it anew. They brought light into darkness. They illuminated just enough of the way forward that we could take another step. It was the kingdom breaking in.

As mentioned, along with Shalene's cancer diagnosis and my son's seizures, my own emotional state fell completely apart: a dark depression, crippling fear, and anxiety. Every day I thought I was dying of something new. I had countless doctor's appointments trying to figure out what was wrong with me. In reality, my body was being bombarded with symptoms of anxiety and worry, but anxiety does not show up on x-rays and ultrasounds. I learned so much about the power of the brain during those months. But most troubling during this time were the various voices I was fighting in my own mind. I do not fully understand where the voices came from or whose they were, but I often heard them. "You are going to die." "You are going to be a single dad." "There is no God." That is what I heard over and over again. Remarkably and mysteriously, Joanne's emails would so often speak directly to a lie I was hearing on a particular day. Without me even telling her, she would call it out, cut if off, and speak truth to move forward. There was no way she could know, but Jesus knew, and he used Joanne over and over again to speak to me and care for me.

Other evenings we spent with Alison in her home. She and her husband, Rod, listened to us talk about our fears and anxieties. And believe me, there were many of them. Some of them were legit while many were completely irrational. But Alison and Rod sat and listened, never judging us or wondering how it was that they got hooked up with a church planter who had serious reservations about his faith and future. They sat and listened the way I believe Jesus sits and listens to us, which I believe, is quite similar to the way I try to sit and listen to my kids when they are hurting, scared, and stressed. They listened with patience, compassion, and kindness. Then they would pray over us. And when Alison prays, things happen. It is like you are in the throne room watching someone take your concerns to the feet of Jesus and laying them at his feet, and then they return to you, communicating Jesus' response. It is an authority couched in humility. There is also always a deep appreciation for who you are in that moment, paired with encouragement to push ahead and to not settle. Alison's prayers always have the Kingdom in sight, like it is just over the horizon waiting to be experienced. Many times she led us into the heart of God and created a space for his hope and power to fall over us in a way that gave life, encouragement, and strength. We made that visit to her home countless times.

What I did not realize at the time was that this was another experience with Jesus as he was teaching me the new way forward. My life and our church needed to embrace this gift that was given to people like Alison and Joanne. Life is one decision after another, one moment of discernment to the next, one possibility of transformation until the day when God's Kingdom will span the universe in full display. Prophets are essential to facilitating these moments along the way the best they can. They are an essential part of showing us the way towards God's full kingdom. I expect I had already experienced the truth and benefits of prophecy before without even knowing it (so it often is with God's mercy and grace), but it was not until I recognized my utter dependency on Jesus that I went intentionally looking for it, named it, and understood the need to give it a place. What became so obvious to myself and others in our church was that we needed these prophets to intentionally share and speak. We were compelled to give them space to lead.

So let us go back to these questions: Do you know who the prophets are in your church? Are they involved in your decision-making processes and day-to-day life as a church? Are they being given opportunities to share what God has placed on their hearts? Are they welcomed as a window into God's preferred future?

Once you know who they are, you must give them a place to be involved, to share, to pray, to speak into decisions and the creation of your church's values. If Jesus is real and the gift of this prophetic imagination — this window into the heart of God — is one of the ways he chooses to presence himself in our church communities, then we must embrace the place of the prophet.

First, you must find them. They are there. I have actually begun to believe that if Jesus starts a church, he will take care of bringing together the pieces to make it work. Remember, the church is his creation. He will provide the foundational core people. There is likely a prophet right under your nose. Or you possibly know who they are, but you are scared to move in this direction. Risk it.

Second, put them to work and help your church community to recognize the gift. I am now in the practice of running ideas, troubles, and dreams past our prophets. Their input and reflection are invaluable. As we began to put together the processes through which we would discern decisions together as a church or shape our guiding values, we have been sure to intentionally create spaces for our prophets to listen, pray, reflect, and share. This collaboration has refined, put the brakes on, and breathed life and energy into ideas. I also ensure that our prophets know my door is always open for them to share what God is putting on their heart. They may not even have a concrete action plan in mind, sometimes they just need to share what they are sensing and seeing. Without fail these experiences are always rich and fruitful. We have also asked our prophets to purposely take issues of discernment — decisions or directions we are considering in our church— to a small group of people learning how to hear the voice of Jesus. In part, this act is prophetic mentorship; it also has shown people that what God is speaking to one person, he is often speaking to everyone, if they will just take the time to listen. Reports from these gatherings are then shared with our leadership team or our whole church. It is fascinating what comes of them. Sometimes the group goes on a Spirit-led rabbit trail that ends up being an encouragement specifically for one person in our community or for us all. Sometimes the group receives great clarity about a decision that the church and our leadership team has been wrestling with for a while. The experience of our prophets can sometimes make a decision simple and easy. On the other hand, sometimes their experiences slow down a decision to refine it, make it better, or close the door completely.

No matter what the outcome, I can honestly say that to this point, the reflection of our prophets regarding any particular discussion or decision has *always* made it better. Every. Single. Time. I always leave these experiences remarking, "Wouldn't you know, it appears Jesus knows what he's doing." He is for us. He will guide us into truth. Our prophets can help us experience these truths as more than just statements but as living reality. Find your prophets and let them into the process. The presence of Jesus exists in that intentionality.

A final word of caution on this topic: it is important to protect your prophets. The temptation to turn them into a fortune teller or dispenser of godly good feelings must be resisted. This will be destructive for all involved and ultimately turn the focus to the prophet rather than the one who is using the prophet to share and speak: Jesus. Within our context we have made the decision to consider carefully in what way our prophets should serve on our leadership team. At times they have, but more often they have not. We keep a close link between the two groups, but I believe it would often be a disservice to our prophets to have them use their energy on some of the more nitty gritty details of church life. Prophets need leadership to be protective of their personal time. Their ability to invest time in their relationship with Jesus is one of the ways they nurture their gifting. If you weigh down your prophet with so much prophetic work (or other jobs) that they cannot spend time with Jesus, you are affectively limiting their gift. Be cautious. Protect them. And finally, encourage them. As mentioned, they bear a heavy burden. Love them. Help them to laugh. Remind them that even small transformations along the way matter. All-out revival is unlikely to happen every day despite

the prophet's desire for it.
Reflecting again on Paul's body metaphor:

We all need each other.
The prophet needs you, too.
Stand with them!

4

Of Robert & Discernment

Do your church's decision-making processes involve Jesus? Do they involve worship, quiet, study of Scriptures, contemplation, prayer, and intentional times of listening to the voice of Jesus?

I have seen or heard of countless forms of decision-making in the local church. Depending on your tradition or denomination, you will have experienced a few different versions of how leadership makes decisions. There are all sorts of methods on the decision-making spectrum. Even within one denomination there can be several different practices used depending on the type of decision being made and who is involved in making it. This, though, has been my observation: many of these methods, no matter the denomination, have a distinctly corporate-America or politically-democratic flavour. Functional leadership of Jesus within many of these models is too often nothing more than window dressing. If our leadership is to really be about Jesus' leadership, then this style of decision-making can be incredibly problematic. If a process operates from an assumption that Jesus is present within the discussion simply because we, as Christians, are involved, or offer a short prayer before we "get started," it falls far short of the potential to experience the living presence and voice of Jesus. Sure, it may happen. Mercy and grace are like that. But my experience has been that explicitly inviting Jesus into these methods and processes and then intentionally giving him space to communicate with and through us paves a far more transformative way forward. Functional leadership is dramatically different than a simple awareness of headship. In Canada our government is technically lead by the King or Queen of England because we are a part of the British Commonwealth. But on a day-to-day basis, that functionally means very little to decision-making. They are not in the room. They do not comment on decisions. We do not want to make Jesus into a symbolic figurehead, despite the fact I am sure he would look great on a coin.

Take, for example, *Robert's Rules of Order.*[1] Many denominations use General Henry Robert's book, or some form of it. If you have never heard of General Robert and his rules, my hunch is that you use a decision-making process that is not dissimilar to the methods put forth in his book. Its influence on governance is wide sweeping across various institutions. First published in 1876, it has been used as a guide to help groups of people make decisions in an orderly fashion. Its original title was the *Pocket Manual of Rules of Order for Deliberative Assemblies.*

---

1 Public Affairs, 2020.

If that sounds a bit like a drill sergeant put it together, that is because it was. Robert was a military man and also a student of parliamentary procedure. The language of the book has a distinctly political and military tone. However, what prompted Robert to write the book in the first place makes for a good tale. As the story goes, Robert was asked to help his local church work through some decisions. The meetings got ugly. Really ugly. People yelled and screamed at each other. There are even some historians who include the throwing of chairs in their retelling. Robert admirably, and with good intentions, desired to bring order and process to the proceedings, so he went to what he knew best: politics and military rule. He wanted people to make decisions in an orderly fashion; he wanted everyone to be heard; and he wanted the majority to have their view succeed. Order, majority rules, and efficient decision-making: these make up the heartbeat of Robert's rules.

Robert wrote his book and established the process in his church. Decisions were able to be made in an orderly and efficient manner. Success! The book took off. Many different organizations started using the model, including more and more churches. Robert travelled across the continent using his methods wherever he went and so the book became a hallmark of organizational process and governance. I will never forget the first time I attended a condo association meeting for the building in which my wife and I once lived. I remember thinking, "We need Robert" as we took two hours to decide on a budget for the flower beds outside. Today the book is in its 12th edition and is still widely regarded as the model of choice for decision-making within local hobby clubs, municipal governments, and churches. It looks great at first glance: order, majority rules, and making decisions in a quick and timely fashion. What is not to love about that? Obviously decisions are a part of life and they can be complicated when groups and organizations are involved (whenever people are involved, really). A tool that helps people make decisions is a good thing. Especially if it stops them from throwing chairs at each other.

But stop here and ask yourself a question. What does that sound like to you? What comes to mind? Do you have the image of Acts 15 in your mind right now? Or do you have the image of a corporate board room or hall of government? If the image you are picturing is of the latter, why then is this the model of choice for many churches? Before you think that is too simplistic a question or observation, let me try and explain my concern.

Four words drive every parent mad while in the car: "Are we there yet?" We all asked that when we were kids. Maybe we still do from time to time. But now that I am a parent I appreciate how ridiculous this question is when asked by a three year-old. How am I supposed to answer? How can I respond in a way that will make sense to my toddler? Do I reply with how many minutes or miles are remaining in the journey? Will my three year-old understand that? Considering one of my three year-old's responses to the question of "What time is it?" is "forty-o-clock," I doubt it. Instead Shalene and I respond by relating the amount of time remaining in the trip to the amount of TV shows it would take to watch before our arrival. That may be an indictment on our parenting, but it works. "We will be there in one episode of *Pound Puppies*." Or "We will be there in the length of time it takes to watch *Frozen*." I still do not know if that actually makes sense to my kid, but it stops him from asking the question at least for five minutes.

When it comes to decision-making, we, like my children on a long trip, are obsessed with the question, "Are we there yet?" People do not like when the process of decision-making takes a long time. This may sound completely counterintuitive and obvious, but in our church, the journey towards a decision has become the point of our decision-making processes. Yes, you read that correctly. Read it again. Stick with me. I want to suggest that in an environment where Jesus is our pastor and leader, the point of entering into a time of decision-making is something other than the decision.

Here is a story with which most of us are quite familiar. In John 6, the disciples go on a trip.

> *When evening came, his disciples went down to the lake, got into a boat, and started across the lake to Capernaum. It was now dark, and Jesus had not yet come to them. The lake became rough because a strong wind was blowing. When they had rowed about three or four miles, they saw Jesus walking on the lake and coming near the boat, and they were terrified. But he said to them, 'It is I; do not be afraid.' Then they wanted to take him into the boat, and immediately the boat reached the land towards which they were going.*
>
> John 6:16-21, NRSV

In the middle of this journey it is safe to assume that the disciples were asking the question, "Are we there yet?" They had jumped in a boat and set out for Capernaum. A storm rolled in. The timeline for their arrival was now out the window and you have to imagine that nervousness, fear, uneasiness, and frustration had taken hold. Then Jesus shows up and immediately they reach their destination.

There are a few odd things about this story. Did skilled fisherman miss that a storm was coming? This was not a quick jaunt across a small pond. They had to know there was a real risk of danger. Why is Jesus not with them when they leave? Why did they set out for Capernaum without him? Why were *followers* leaving without their leader? The story only notes that Jesus was not with them yet. The sky darkened and a storm set in, and Jesus was not with them yet. There appears to be an expectation that he would be with them, though initially he was not. I believe that the disciples left for Capernaum without Jesus because he told them to do so. It seems like Jesus must have said, "Go, and I will catch up." That certainly fits the *modus operandi* of a relationship between a Rabbi and disciple. He gives the orders; they obey. And by this time they must have become somewhat accustomed to Jesus' seemingly bizarre commands (e.g. In the story just prior to this episode, Jesus tells his disciples to do some remarkable things with a few loaves of bread.) Jesus makes requests that do not always make a lot of sense, but what follows these requests is nothing short of miraculous. I think Jesus said something like this to the disciples: "Get in the boat and go to Capernaum. I know it sounds weird because it is getting dark, but I will catch up." How was he going to catch up? Would he get his own boat? It had to seem like a strange directive, but they did it. They got in the boat and set out on the water at dusk.

Then *two* miracles take place. Growing up there was only one miracle in this story as I read it: Jesus walking on water. What I had not noticed was that as soon as Jesus shows up whilst walking on water in the midst of a rough storm, the boat arrives at its destination. Until this point we are led to believe that the disciples' boat is aimlessly crashing around in the storm, miles from shore. Miracle one: Jesus walks on water and arrives on the scene. Miracle two: When it seemed as though the disciples were lost in the storm, they arrive at their destination. Poof! When Jesus shows up on the journey, they arrive at their destination. The point, then, is the encounter with Jesus. When Jesus arrives so, too, does the destination. What initially felt like the point — getting to Capernaum — is replaced with a new miraculous and mysterious experience that teaches a new point. Jesus said go. The disciples did. Then he showed them that when they met him on the journey, they would also reach their destination; they would realize the *real* point. The point was meeting with Jesus. They still ended up where they needed to be, but the climax of the story was their encounter with Jesus.

I have asked "Are we there yet?" in far more circumstances than just car trips. In the midst of decision-making and discernment I have asked that question many times. I do this because I am convinced that the point is getting to the decision. In our churches we enter into the process of decision-making believing that determining a resolution is the point. To help us, we use tools like Robert's Rules. Why not? As western people, highly influenced by the logic and working of democratic institutions, we implicitly believe in values like "majority rules." We like order; we dislike chaos. And we are the 24-minute sitcom solution society; all of our problems and challenges can be solved in 30 minutes with commercial breaks. But all of this misses the point. The point is the journey wherein we meet with Jesus. If we adopt methods that do not intentionally and explicitly make this the point, we can miss Jesus and seriously miss out on what he offers us. He is the one that will transform us, lead us, and guide us. Realizing that our purpose can be to learn and hear from Jesus we can reframe discernment and decision-making as an opportunity to meet with Jesus wherein the decision is a bonus outcome. We obediently endeavour into a decision-making process when the Spirit prompts us, but the decision itself becomes of secondary value. The primary value is to be shaped by Jesus by letting him call the shots.

Reframing this process in this way does a variety of things. First, it always helps to keep the decision, whatever it might be, in perspective. It is not the most important part of the process. Second, it provides an opportunity for discipleship within a process that is often looked upon as something to avoid. I have a few odd friends who find Robert's Rules exciting and cannot wait for their next opportunity to wade into a decision-making process. However, if the opportunity is presented where within this process we get to experience the mysterious power of Christ, this is a game-changer. If we get into the boat with the promise that Jesus will meet us in the journey, I am far more inclined to get in the boat despite the darkness and storm on the horizon. This new perspective also helps us to remember that discernment and decisions do not have to come quickly. I appreciate that sometimes we have time-sensitive decisions to be made, but often when we think we must hurry up, Jesus has a way of slowing things down for the sake of teaching and stretching us. When your leader is the one who sits on the throne, you can take comfort in his timeline. It is a matter of trust and an exercise in faith. If Jesus needs it to go quickly, he will push ahead. If he is aware that a decision is not as urgent as we may think, he will (often) slow us down to make room for teaching along the way.

I am sure that one reason we gravitate towards a system like Robert's Rules is because it eliminates risk and gives us a safe and orderly structure from which to work. This is not a bad thing, unless the fear of risk is, as I have already mentioned, rooted in our inability to trust that Jesus is for us and will presence himself in our midst. Sadly, I think this fear is all too common, which is why I believe Jesus can be intentionally ignored in the process. Giving up control to him is too scary. We trust General Robert's rules instead because they are surefire and easy. Using Robert's methods can work often enough, too. But the point here is about missed chances. Sure, you can get a decision with a method like Robert's Rules, but you may then miss the opportunity for transformation in a variety of forms.

What is the way forward, then? I do not believe we need to throw out everything we have been doing. Instead, we must reimagine how we can invite Jesus to lead us and transform us in many of the practices and methods we currently use. When it comes to the idea of decision-making, I believe there is a great opportunity to tweak and adapt. We likely do not need to start from scratch.

General Robert may still be of use to us, but let us begin with the premise that our process must *first* be influenced by the Spirit and *then* helped by other aides instead of the other way around.

In the mid-sixteenth century, Ignatius of Layola produced a piece of writing that came to be known as *The Spiritual Exercises*. It is a collection of resources focused on deepening one's journey with God. The resources lend themselves to practices of meditation, discernment, decision-making, and sensing God's will. Followers of Ignatius adapted his work to be used for these purposes, both personally and corporately. If you have ever heard the terms "consolation" and "desolation" when it comes to discernment, these are Ignatian principles.

While Catholic and Orthodox folks have never forgotten Ignatius, it has only been recently that Evangelicals have returned to his methods. Interestingly, my only experience with Ignatius' work during my theological education in the late 90's was in theology, church history, and personal spirituality classes. He never came up in leadership classes. I do not recall ever hearing his name mentioned in all the leadership conferences that were front and centre back then. Thankfully this is changing.

Leaders and authors like Ruth Haley Barton have done some excellent work bringing Ignatian spirituality out of "personal devotions" time and back into methods and practices of leadership and decision-making. Her book, *Pursuing God's Will Together: A*

Discernment Practice for Leadership Groups,[2] focuses entirely on this valuable on Ignatius' writings as an applicable resource. It is a wonder we Evangelicals lost sight of this resource. It is again the great irony of a supposed Jesus-centric evangelicalism.

Consider Ignatius' work on discernment in this way: it is a method for coming to a decision in an orderly fashion that invites the presence of Jesus to manifest himself as the primary aim of the process. You make a decision, but you pursue Jesus in the process. You invite him in. You intentionally surrender the process and your will to his will. If that sounds great, it is! It begins with a more charismatic understanding of decision-making as the means by which we can know the heart of God than many evangelicals may feel comfortable with. A false proposition is that the more charismatic the process the more chaotic it must be. That is simply not true. Ignatius' work helped to develop a variety of methods that remain orderly and really quite simple to follow. The type-A personalities in your midst can still be satisfied. And a bonus: it is highly unlikely that chairs will be thrown. At every step along the way Ignatius' guiding principles makes the focus about Jesus and his capacity to break into the conversation to shape and mould the process. It puts people in a posture of receiving and setting aside their own agenda. It is also fundamentally different from the democratic principal of majority rules. It attempts to breathe to life consensus because it operates from an assumption that Jesus desires unity for his church (more on this to come). If you have never seen Ignatius' work, I suggest you find it. There are wonderful resources out there that have

---

2 IVP Books, 2012.

simplified the work into easy-to-follow guides.[3]

Jim Manney at *Ignatian Spirituality* provides a simple breakdown of Ignatius' process for discernment. While I do suggest you find the resource to see the full breakdown, I will provide the transcript below for a few of the sections.[4]

---

1. Identify the decision to be made or the issue to be resolved.

2. Formulate the issue in a proposal.

3. Pray for openness to God's will, and for freedom from prejudgment and addictions.

Ask for that inner freedom and balance that allows you not to be inclined more toward one alternative or option than to the other. This means to ask to be free enough to be influenced only by this one value: which alternative will give most glory to God and be expressive of my own deepest self, my authentic self?

To arrive at this absolutely necessary inner freedom, you may wish to discuss the matter with a spiritually mature person who can help you. In particular, discuss what obstacles could be limiting your freedom by blocking you or inclining you to one alternative

---

[3] You can find some helpful examples here: www.ignatianspirituality.com & www.transformingcenter.org

[4] www.ignatianspirituality.com/making-good-decisions/an-approach-to-good-choices/an-ignatian-framework-for-making-a-decision/

over the other.

Possible obstacles: projections, disordered attachments like inferiority complexes, superiority complexes, or glorified self-images; "shoulds" or "oughts" that tyrannize you; perfectionism, fears, materialistic greed, and possessiveness; past hurts and self-pity; competitiveness that leads to envy; impatience with yourself or others; lust, ingratitude, and irreverence; desire for control, power, status, prestige, exclusiveness, and so forth.

As preparation for your prayer, read over slowly, carefully, and attentively the following Scripture passages:

Luke 17:5-6
Luke 12:22-32
Matthew 13:44-46
Matthew 14:22-33
Luke 18:35-43
Mark 10:17-22
Matthew 5:13-16
Luke 14:33
2 Timothy 1:7
Matthew 7:24-25
Luke 16:13
Philippians 3:7-10
Luke 11:5-13
Matthew 20:26-28

Note the passages that strike you most strongly. Make these passages the source from which you talk with God about the particular areas where you need freedom. Where do you need greater detachment about the alternatives or options in your proposal? Bring them to God in prayer. Ask above all for a deep love: love for God, for the people being affected by the decision, and for your own true self or authentic self. Pray that no self-centered attraction or aversion about a choice will sidetrack you from what the Holy Spirit is pointing you to. Ask for the guidance of the Holy Spirit in all this.

4. Gather all the necessary information.

Find out all the relevant specifics relating to the decision: Who? What? Where? When? How much? Why? Be satisfactorily informed.

Be sure to consult with everyone who will be intimately affected by the decision being made: spouse, children, other family, friends, colleagues. Get their input about it, including their feelings and desires.

Discuss this matter with someone sensitive to Christian spiritual values. This could be a friend, counselor, priest, or minister—someone who will be honest and objective with you. Discuss the matter in detail—its values and possibilities, your strengths and weaknesses.

5. Repeat the third step: Pray for openness to God's will.

Pray about the matter again in light of the data you have gathered and the counsel of others. Most likely new feelings and desires have been stirred up that need to be shared with God so that they might be purified of any prejudgment or disordered attachment. This is a "freedom check." Are you free enough to be influenced only by this one value: which alternative will give most glory to God and be expressive of your own deepest self, your authentic self?

6. State all the reasons for and all the reasons against each alternative in the proposal.

7. Do a formal evaluation of all the advantages and disadvantages.

Repeat Step 3, praying for openness and freedom. Pray for light about factors that inhibit freedom and openness to God. Are there any? Beg God for the help to be detached from disordered attachments that might be influencing you. Pray for a deeper faith in God and love for God.

Evaluate the advantages and disadvantages by asking two questions:

Which option more evidently leads to God's service and better serves the growth of your true self in the Holy Spirit?

Which option seems more consistent with your own faith journey and history with God?

8. Observe the direction of your will while reflecting on the advantages and disadvantages.

As you evaluate the choices, your desires will be influenced by the Holy Spirit; that is, your will becomes more inclined toward one option and less inclined toward the other. These inclinations may fluctuate between options. Pay attention to these inner movements. Pray for light from the Holy Spirit about them. Eventually, your will is likely to focus on one of the alternatives.

If your will does not settle on one choice but continues to fluctuate between the two, a disordered attachment may be influencing you. This is a signal to do some more prayer. Return to Step 3. Ask God to free you from any selfish inclinations and lead you to worthy motives. Pray that the Holy Spirit draws your will and its desires to God's will.

9. Ask God to give you feelings of consolation about the preferred option.

This is the third of three states of the discernment. First, you asked the Holy Spirit to transform your thoughts (listing advantages and disadvantages). Second, you asked the Holy Spirit to transform your desires (your will) while evaluating the lists of advantages and disadvantages. Now you ask the Holy Spirit to stir feelings of spiritual consolation. These are feelings of joy, enthusiasm, deeper faith, greater hope and trust, greater love, confidence, courage. These thoughts, desires, and feelings are all parts of your inner experience of the Holy Spirit guiding you to the truth.

These feelings of consolation accompany your desires when

they are clearly pointed toward loving and serving God, others, and your true self. They are very different from the feelings that accompany your desires when they are influenced by disordered attachments aimed only at your selfish ways.

If your feelings fluctuate between consolation and desolation, you may be under the influence of mixed motives and disordered attachments.

If so, return to Step 3: pray for freedom and openness to God.

10. Trust in God and make your decision, even if you are not certain about it.

11. Confirm the decision.

Not your run of the mill board meeting is it? In my experience, Ignatius' guiding principles present a stark contrast to most of the models of decision-making and discernment to which I contributed in my early days of ministry.

If your first inclination is to think, "That would take forever!" You are right, it could. But I want to remind you of what we have already discussed: efficiency is not the point. Adopting a process like this when you have been used to a more familiar process will take time to embrace and it will be a matter of education for those involved. It will, however, open up all kinds of new possibilities for discipleship, growth, and experiences of Jesus' presence. We want to make good decisions and we want to experience and be transformed by Jesus, do we not? Why would we pass up the opportunity to shape our methods in a way that aides achieving both of those desires? Why would we proclaim to be the church empowered by the Spirit and then deny the opportunity to invite the Spirit into our processes?

The 18th-century English minister, John Wesley, also has something to contribute to this discussion. In much of Wesley's theological work he emphasizes the use of four principals in establishing theological positions or beliefs. Though Wesley never gave a snappy title to his work, this process was eventually formed by his followers into what we now call, "The Wesleyan Quadrilateral." Many books have been written explaining Wesley's thoughts and process in great detail. I have found Don Thorsen's book on this subject to be most helpful.[5]

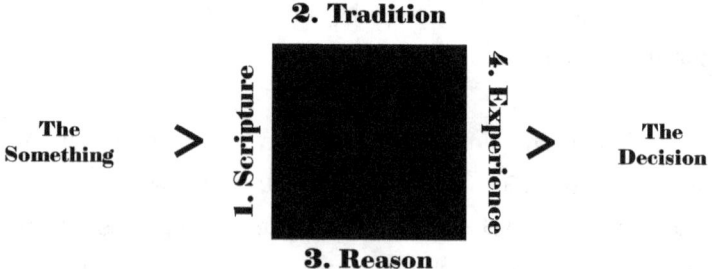

---

5 *The Wesleyan Quadrilateral: An Introduction.* Emeth Press, 2018.

Wesley proposes a basic premise that our discernment as Christians ought to be put through four categories of testing, thought, and discussion. They are **1. Scripture, 2. Tradition, 3. Reason, and 4. Experience.** We start with something: a thought, belief, a decision to be made, or an idea. Next, we work that *something* through each side of the quadrilateral, starting with Scripture, Tradition, Reason, and finally Experience.

Scripture is perhaps the easiest of the four for those of us who are Evangelicals to get our head around. Our *modus operandi* is to head to the Bible, as we should. We take our something and we hold it against Scripture, seeking to be informed, to find insight and to find guidance. We know that the Bible is not a manual or roadmap, and we know that it does not speak to all of life's questions, but as we enter into the story of God and his people, we submit our will and that something to the grand narrative. Scripture *will* speak to our *something*, but maybe not with a proof text. (More on reading the Bible later.)

The second quadrilateral principal is one with which many Evangelicals struggle: the capital "T" **Tradition** of the Christian faith. From the book of Acts, through all the great councils and creeds, through the Fathers and Mothers of the Church, through our faith's greatest theologians, monks, preachers, servants, saints, and official documents, we ask what the living tradition of the church has said about our *something*. We capitalize the word "Tradition" because she is alive. She is a voice that speaks to us from centuries past, and she is filled with wisdom and the blood, sweat, dirt, and tears of real life.

Without doubt, the Reformation and its descendants have shaped many Protestants with a degree of skepticism, doubt, and even vitriol regarding the history of the church prior to 1600. To my friends and peers who struggle with this, I invite you to do two things: go for a drink with your local Catholic, Orthodox, or Anglican priest(s). Get to know them. First, start by celebrating the fact that you all believe Jesus has been resurrected from the grave and you believe he is Lord. That is *always* a good place to start. And then ask them about their hopes for their church and their people. Ask them about their own journey into faith with Jesus. Ask them about what they love and dislike about their respective traditions. My hunch is you will soon find an ally in the faith. And then you can begin to see the beauty of her: the living bride of Christ. She has been around for over 2,000 years. She has seen and experienced much. And she has something to say to your *something*. Second, I highly recommend reading D.H. Williams' book, *Retrieving the Tradition and Renewing Evangelicalism: A Primer for Suspicious Protestants*.[6] Williams provides an excellent counter to the belief which many Evangelicals hold that the church more or less disappeared between the age of Constantine and the Reformation. It turns out she did not.

Then we come to Wesley's application of **Reason**. We use our brains. We think. We reflect. We honour the God who gave us the ability to think and discern by doing just that (Isaiah 1:18). We follow the advice of James and we ask for wisdom and then use it (James 1:5). We vigorously discuss and debate. We invite critique. We listen to and consider multiple voices. We take the

---

6 Wm. B. Eerdmans Publishing Co., 1999.

time to contemplate. Our Protestant upbringing has turned many of us into excellent debaters and thinkers.

Finally, we acknowledge that **Experience** shapes who we are and that it informs our *something*. The Spirit uses our feelings — *our gut* — and within our real life experiences, she informs us. Unfortunately modernity shaped a skepticism toward this principal and turned it into more of an addendum than the great beautiful surprise and illumination at the end of the quadrilateral journey. In fact, it is in this principal we find a unique opportunity to incorporate Ignatian principals coupled with our desire to be led by Jesus.

To facilitate this, I turn to the work of Lee, my friend from the coffee shop. Lee began as my professor in seminary, became a friend, and as previously mentioned, is now a mentor and active member in our church community. His friendship, encouragement, and wisdom have been invaluable to me as a leader and in my own spiritual formation.

In seminary (and life in general) Lee teaches theological reflection. He uses the *Wesleyan Quadrilateral* as one of the means to provide students with a framework for how to do theological reflection. But over the years, and because of much of what has thus far been discussed in this book, he began to tinker with the model. Instead of having Experience be the caboose on the four car train (which implies least in significance), he moved it to the beginning.

Rightly so, I believe, Lee insists that the primary question we ought to be asking is "What is the Spirit saying now?" That is our starting place. From there, with that question and hope of experience in mind, we work through the other principals. If Jesus is to be our pastor, teacher, and guide, then we should begin with the assumption and practice that he will lead us through the process, illuminating and speaking as we move along.

Someday I am sure Lee and Wesley will have a good chat about this in the coffeeshop of Heaven.

In our church we have created something that draws from Barton, Ignatius, Robert's Rules, Wesley, Beach, and other conceptions we made up ourselves along the way. I am not here claiming that what we have done is perfect, but I do believe it is a step in the best direction. We use prayer, worship, meditation, reflection, study, sharing, discussion, Scripture, listening prayer; we take all the time necessary to work through the process, not being afraid to say "We are not there yet." Since creating this process we have used it many times. It has had its bumps in the road and we have had to figure out how to use a new process like this while still meeting some of the requirements for decision-making prescribed by our denomination. That has required creativity, and some grace and patience on the part of our denomination's leadership (for which I am very grateful). Depending on your denominational structure, this may be more difficult than it has been for us. Or it could be easier. Either way, my advice is to keep pushing ahead. Figure out ways to be creative. Ask Jesus what you should do. Because despite the bumps along the way, what we have learned in our church by adopting this multi-layered process is that Jesus does not fail — he makes himself known.

This process has become another confirmation that Jesus is alive and he is for us. To this point we have not experienced anything like the Transfiguration in our gatherings of discernment, but we have without doubt known the presence of Jesus and his voice as we intentionally bring him into the equation. When we felt like a decision would be very difficult or divisive, our process has given Jesus the opportunity to form unity. Sometimes Jesus has slowed us down and redirected us to a place we were not heading. And very often, in a process like this, Jesus uses different avenues of communication through all sorts of people to communicate his desire for us. Young and old, whether mature or new in the faith: Jesus will communicate through those who earnestly create space and expectation for his presence. I believe he loves to do this in the midst of our diverse communities as a way of demonstrating his unity, economy, gospel, and Kingdom. The many different forms of interaction with Jesus in a process like this create space for introvert and extrovert, shy and bombastic, artist and mathematician, to join the process, be involved, and to experience Jesus — and to be discipled — in the process. Which sounds more inviting? "Come to our business meeting where we use Robert's Rules to carefully make a decision," or "Come to our decision-making process where we meet with Jesus." I would take the latter. Every. Single. Time.

Here is the basic rundown of what we do when it comes to discernment and decision-making. We use variations of this template in all situations: whole church, leadership team, committee groups, and wherever else we make decisions.

The Leadership Team (LT) operates with the assumption that the Spirit can and will lead to truth, consensus, and a process for moving forward. This happens through prayerful discernment, discussion, debate, Scripture-searching, and consultation with the Tradition. This belief, however, does not dismiss the possibility that risks and experiments may fail. However, this belief does mean that even in the failures, the "failed" process and relationships within the LT and church are still of value and are in the midst of being shaped and transformed to look more like Jesus.

Together, the LT prayerfully discusses pertinent big-picture issues related to the church's vision and mission. When the LT comes to Spirit-led consensus on issues, it presents the issues to the church for discernment. This is not permission-seeking, but rather an opportunity for continued discernment of the Spirit's leading.

If the discernment process leads to indecision, the LT will assume that they did not explain things properly, missed something, require more clarity in the topic, or need to see the indecision as a caution or "no" from the Spirit. In this case, the LT will re-discuss the issue and either return to the church with a reconstructed presentation, drop the issue altogether, or leave it to be picked up at a later date.

If the discernment process leads to a decision, the LT will take appropriate action.

The Process

1. Pick the issue

1a. Present a subject or choice for discernment. Depending on the subject or choice, the framing and presentation may be done by the pastor alone, the Leadership Team alone, the entire church, or various collaborations of the aforementioned.

1b. To begin, the group asks, "Spirit, is now the time to discuss (insert subject or choice here) for discernment?"

2. Ironing out the issue

2a. Why are we thinking about doing this? Ask this question as it relates to the church's Guiding Values and the voice of Jesus in the church's midst: i.e., the why. Do not ask this question as it relates to an achieved outcome: i.e., the how and what. We want to be vine-focussed, not fruit-focussed at this point in the process.

A time of worship, prayer, praise, or thanksgiving may be appropriate at this time.

2b. Are we indifferent to all but what God would say to us and have us do? Are we willing to lay our agenda down as we engage this process of discernment? Are we denouncing fear?

2c. What are the biblical texts or images that come to mind as we begin this process? What dreams and visions come to mind? What does the Tradition of the Church say to us? What is Jesus saying to us?

3. Moulding the issue

3a. Pray in silence for _____ minutes, asking the Spirit to tell us from who we need to hear. Whose voices are we to hear? Who can bring us clarity and wisdom on this issue?

If the Spirit is directing you towards listening to someone our society may deem "the least of these," take special note. The voice of Jesus is often heard in the marginalized.

> **The discernment process may pause here for as long as necessary.**

3b. What are the possible options or paths within this subject or choice? Brainstorm. List. Put everything on the table no matter how crazy it sounds.

3c. Now improve upon each option. Make each the best it can be.

4. Choices

4a. Weigh the options using the following disciplines:

Does the Spirit lure us?

Does Scripture speak to an option with imagery or story?

Vigorous mental examination

List the fruits

Do you feel consolation or desolation?

> **The discernment process may pause here for as long as necessary.**

4b. Are we ready to bring this to a decision? Or do we need more time for reflection, prayer, study, or research? Or do we not feel like the best possible option is on the table? Judge the response.

5. Decision time

5a. Is it clear to us how we should proceed?

People can respond as follows:

> **I like this the way it's been stated.**
> *(Consensus achieved)*

> **I am concerned, but will support this decision.**
> *(Consensus achieved)*

> **I am uneasy, but will stand aside.**
> *(Consensus achieved)*

> **I cannot support this the way it has been stated.**
> *(Non-Consensus)*

If seriously divided, not there yet, or at an impasse:

> *Revisit the subject or choice*
> *and practice 2b again.*

> *or*

> *Take time for further prayer and reflection.*
> *Set a time and a follow-up discussion.*

> *or*
> *Appoint someone to decide for the group.*

or

Count only the "yes" votes.

or

Drop the issue entirely or for a time.

6. How do you feel?

Test your heart.

Do you feel consolation or desolation?
Are we good to move on?

To function effectively, especially as a new process, it is crucial to disciple people in listening prayer and to be open to the different ways in which God chooses to communicate. Yes, God can choose to communicate through a majority-rules voting process, but he may also communicate through Scripture, images, dreams, visions, or simply a sense of some feeling in our gut. This process must be nurtured and given space in our churches so that when we enter into times of discernment, our people are prepared to see and hear Jesus in a variety of ways. This is why the process must include more than one mode of sensing and hearing the presence of Jesus. Learning how to discern the voice of Jesus is key. What does he sound like? How do we know it is him communicating and not other principalities? How do we evaluate what we sense or hear? These are all important questions which involve intentional discipleship, exercise, and training. They do not, however, all need to be perfectly understood before venturing down this road. As mentioned, the beauty of a process like this is that it is a form of discipleship in itself. You may not always get it right. But if the premise is that Jesus is with us, for us, and wants us to get this right, we can take comfort that in our pursuit of this sort of model, he will hold our hand along the way. Be smart. Use wisdom. Discern. But do not be afraid to risk as you move forward.

I want to look like a people who believe Jesus is alive. I want to demonstrate my literal dependency on his voice and leading. I want those in my church to see me pointing to Jesus as our pastor. I want non-Christians to look in the room while this is happening and see just how crazy seriously we take all of this. If a non-Christian looks in the room and cannot see the difference between what we do and how the local hobby club makes decisions, something is wrong. I know it may feel risky. I know it will feel strange at first. You might even encounter a storm in the dark along the way. The disciples in John 6 no doubt surely had some reservations and words for Jesus after they got lost in the middle of the lake. But when Jesus comes and says, "I am; do not be afraid," everything changes. The destination is found in that moment. On the journey, the encounter with Jesus becomes the point of realization. Our aim in the process is Jesus: to see him, hear his voice, and have him lead us.

**When Jesus has met with us,
however it is that he chooses to do so,
we will have arrived.**

AS YOU CONSIDER NEW MODELS
FOR DISCERNMENT,
THINK ON THESE QUESTIONS:

1. How are you inviting people to hear from Jesus?

2. How are you inviting people to experience Jesus?

3. How are you inviting people to see Jesus as their pastor and leader in the midst of the process?

4. How are you inviting people to expect his presence in tangible ways, as an active person in the room with things to say and contribute?

5

Can Jesus Lead You to Consensus?

Acts 15 is really *the* story of discernment. I think it is the most remarkable moment in the history of the church. Imagine today a group of Bishops within the upper hierarchy of the Roman Catholic Church — not a group of outsiders — go to the Pope and suggest, "We think the Roman Catholic Church should stop requiring people to take part in the Eucharist." Imagine a group of Eastern Orthodox Bishops suggesting to the Patriarch that baptism no longer be part of the church's practice. Imagine the presidents of several large Protestant denominations get together one day and suggest to their peers that they have a hunch that preaching is no longer that important in the planning of a Sunday service. In each of these scenarios someone would be laughed out of the room, or worse. And I think what Paul suggests to Peter in Acts 15 is more shocking than any of these fictitious examples I have put forward. Make no mistake, it was *crazy* for Paul to enter that room and suggest to Peter and the others that circumcision was no longer needed to be a part of the Jewish and the new Christian tradition. Circumcision was an order from the mouth of God himself — a way of life. It was as great an identity marker to the Jewish faith as was the promised land or the temple. It had existed as a divine ritual for centuries. And Paul walks into the room that day and says, "Yeah...I don't think we need to do this anymore." If there were ever the makings for disunity, it was then and there. But as we know, that did not occur. A remarkable statement in the letter sent to the churches after that discussion stands as a hopeful beacon for all matters of discernment.

For it has seemed good to the Holy Spirit and to us to impose on you no further burden than these essentials.

Acts 15:28, NRSV

In one historical moment, that group of people reshaped the essentials. People with opposing views on a monumental issue embarked on a process of discernment together and, by the power of the Holy Spirit, found unity. No vote. No majority rules. Rather, unity. Consensus. The transformational shift within the church because of this moment cannot be understated. The fact that the church remained unified through that crucial example of discernment was quite literally an act of divine intervention. This early church created a space for the Spirit to breathe to life unity, and she did. People *should* have been throwing chairs at each other during the process. It had to have been a heated discussion. And sure, there were still some bumps and bruises along the way between the gentile and Jewish Christians. But in this process of discernment, with all its potential for divisiveness, chaos, anger, hurt feelings, and brokenness, the Spirit formed a unity that ought to make us marvel and give us hope for how it could be in our churches.

I do not imagine that most of our churches are discussing issues as weighty as was discussed in Acts 15. But we often come together to make decisions. Who will serve on our leadership teams? What will we do with our money? In what sorts of activities will we involve our church? What kind of guiding values do we want to have as a church? Forks in the road come up from time to time where we have to make a decision that will alter the future of our congregation in a meaningful way. For many of us, we use discernment and decision-making tools that end with a vote where the majority wins and the minority loses. Sometimes we have the pleasure of having a decision made with 100% approval, but that is not always the case.

Can churches embark on acts of decision-making and discernment with an operating assumption that consensus is possible? If the Spirit can bring consensus in Acts 15, can we not trust her to do so in the life of our church? When Paul asks us to pursue the bond of unity in Ephesians, I have to believe that he can make such a bold challenge because he has witnessed first-hand the capability of the Spirit to breathe unity into the most divisive of situations.

I know what you are thinking. The New Testament has a few stories where unity could not be found. True. Paul himself seemed unable to come to unity on an issue with his one-time friend, Barnabas. But we cannot let the reality of brokenness ever be the starting point for our models. It is true that the brokenness of creation affects everything. As Christians, though, we ought to be defined by a hope that each story has the promise of the Spirit's interaction, redemption, reconciliation, and outbreaking. Let us begin from the belief that Jesus is with us, for us, and wanting to guide us. Remember that he is our pastor and he is in the room. He is victorious. Why not start from a position that assumes we can take Jesus at his word? He will send *The Companion* who will guide those of us who submit to him into truth.

I have had this conversation about consensus and the processes for getting there with many church leaders and I often get the same response: "That sounds like the ideal, but it will never work." Honestly, the lack of hope infuriates me. The people who say this are the same people who believe Jesus rose from the dead and is alive right now. And what on earth does that have to do with anything, you ask? Let me go back to the idea of being crazy from a couple of chapters ago. If you are crazy enough to believe in an implausible act like resurrection, then why can you not believe that the one who you believe is resurrected can be taken seriously? This is the same guy who said, "Tear down the temple and I'll rebuild it in three days." That seemed ridiculous, but then he showed us he could do it. He said he would send the Spirit to guide us into truth, to knit us together as the Body of Christ. Then the Spirit provided us with an incredible example of this working in Acts 15. What, I ask, is the difference? Do we believe it or not? Belief does not mean we do not have moments of disbelief; faith is hard. But if we can ask our churches to celebrate Easter each year, why can we not ask them to enter into decision-making and discernment believing that unity is possible, even the expectation, at the end of the process? And if we can do that, then let us embrace methods that provide opportunity for consensus rather than those in which one side wins and the other loses. It is worth noting that never does a vote take place again in the New Testament after Pentecost. The last variation of one on record is when the disciples draw straws to replace Judas. It seems the New Testament church had a new form of discernment and practice after the Spirit arrives on the scene.

It is at this point I will follow up my questions regarding knowing who your prophets are and assessing your decision making models with a third inquiry.

How does consensus work in your processes and methods? Can we work from an assumption that despite our brokenness, Jesus wants us to achieve unity and consensus?

A few years ago I was asked to join a group, which had been commissioned by our denomination and its president, to work on a particularly divisive issue. It was not a creedal issue — we were not debating the divinity or humanity of Jesus — but it was an issue with deeply held beliefs and practices within our particular tradition of the Christian faith. There were eight of us in the group, four on one side of the issue and four on the other side. It had caused all sorts of pain within our denomination for people on either side. We were given a simple task: to find a way forward in unity. Okay, so it was not simple at all. In fact, at our first face-to-face meeting, our chair asked us to go around the table one by one and to talk about our hope in being able to find a way forward. Every single one of us, including the chair, spoke from a posture of fear, worry, and hurt. Not one of us believed there was a way we could achieve the task that was put before us. Most of us did not even want to be there because we held so little hope. The honesty was illuminating and helpful, but it was certainly not how anyone would choose to script such a moment. Here we were, all Christians of deep faith, unable to muster the faith to believe that this was a possible task.

Our group met for several months, sometimes face to face, sometimes over teleconference, and often through email communication. Each person did their best to minimize debating their position, since we all were keenly aware that both positions on either side of the issue were deeply held. No one was going to change their mind because of debate. There were no new arguments or perspectives to share. People were entrenched (a horrible but somewhat accurate military term to use in this situation). Besides, out-debating one another was not our mandate. We were supposed to find a way to move forward into unity, while knowing we would remain diverse in our held beliefs. This made the challenge even more difficult. Unity in the midst of diversity: how?

But a shift began to occur within our group several months into working together. During our second face-to-face meeting, after a morning of prayer together, something changed. We were trying to grapple with how to find a way forward, discussing how to shape some sort of statement that would both acknowledge each position as possible and workable, while suggesting that neither belief had the corner on an absolute truth. Working towards this goal led to a defining moment. Exasperated, one of the participants said in a raised voice: "But I think your position is wrong, and I cannot concede that my position could be wrong!" Until this point we had been trying to wordsmith a statement that hinged on everyone's ability to speak humbly from their particular position. Problematically, however, as this scenario illustrates, a statement like this fails to acknowledge that a person may be so certain in their position that they cannot fathom backing down. They believe they are *right*. Their theology has both informed their decision and become shaped by it. To say "I could be wrong," which sounds humble and honourable, is actually dishonest and downplays the hard work and wrestling the person has done in arriving at their conclusion. One should not be arrogant in a position they hold, but holding to a principal is not wrong.

The speaker then followed up their initial remark: "But I believe that Jesus is alive and that he wins and that he is coming back someday. And I believe you believe that. And when that day comes, none of this will matter the way we think it does now. We will all stand before the Lamb unified in his presence. And because we can find unity in the person of Jesus, I can happily stand before you and say 'you're wrong,' but move forward with you in unity." And that statement changed everything. We would not be able to wordsmith unity into reality. We would not be able to create unity on an issue that was not creedal and where people held different understandings that mattered deeply to them. Rather, we found unity in the person of Jesus. This may sound like a hokus pokus moment, but we truly started to sense him at the table with us. We would often point to a space in the room as if he were standing there; we would point to the space and say, "Him. Our unity is in *him*." We found our unity and it was Jesus. Please do not read that and think to yourself that it is too easy, too simplistic, or too child-like. It was incredibly powerful, complex, mysterious, and divine. Trying to write this now is difficult, because I really do not know how to put words to the experience our group began to have together from that time onwards. Jesus met us. The Spirit presenced herself in our midst. Unlike the Acts 15 story, we did not emerge from that time together with a unified theological position on the issue at hand, but we did emerge with a unified experience of Jesus that enabled us to help our denomination chart a new way forward. We all agreed on it. We found consensus. We never voted because we did not need to.

Our hope is in Jesus. This means that our personal convictions, which do and ought to matter a great deal to us, must be lived out in recognition that as a whole, we are all people who are pursuing Jesus, and placing our hope in his current and ultimate victory. This is liberating. When Jesus is our hope — when our trust lies in him — we are freed to disagree while remaining unified. We are freed to work things out in gracious community. Our operating assumption must be that those with whom we disagree have their ultimate hope in Jesus and that they are pursuing him in the midst of their reasoning, discussions, and decisions. Undoubtedly, seeking unity can be complicated, and it requires a Spirit-infused humility, grace, and patience within all participants. Our convictions are directly linked to what we believe is a faithful interpretation of Jesus' voice and Word. However, Christian traditions throughout history have demonstrated that good-hearted, Christ-following members can have competing convictions while they simultaneously submit these convictions to the greater cause and awareness of pursuing and experiencing Jesus and his mission in the world. It must sound so sweet to Jesus when his people leave a process of discernment by saying in unity, "It seems good to us and the Holy Spirit that we...".

In our church's process we have what we call four levels of consensus. We enter into each time of discernment with everyone knowing that our decision will be framed in this way and that our goal and belief is that the Spirit will guide us towards consensus and unity. From the moment we begin, everyone knows that our expectation is Spirit-infused consensus. Not uniformity. Not even total agreement, but consensus that breathes life into unity that only the Spirit can nurture and sustain.

As I already shared, the process we use is aimed at achieving consensus in a decision. People can respond as follows when it comes to decision time:

I like this the way it's been stated.
(Consensus achieved)

I am concerned, but will support this decision.
(Consensus achieved)

I am uneasy, but will stand aside.
(Consensus achieved)

I cannot support this the way it has been stated.
(Non-Consensus)

If we remain seriously divided after asking people to align with one of these four categories, we circle back into the process. The beauty of the process, though, is that by the time we get to these choices, the feeling of consensus is already in the room. I believe it is a demonstration of the Spirit with us. I must be honest with you, though; we are a small church. We have never had more than fifty people involved in one of these discernment processes. It is only fair that I tell you that, because I want to acknowledge that the more people you involve in this sort of exercise the harder it will become. So this is as good a place as any to say a few things about the sizes of our churches.

I believe that nurturing the presence of Jesus as our pastor, and all that we have discussed so far, is easier with a smaller group. This leads me to suggest that smaller churches are more ideal than larger churches. And this perspective upsets people. The big church pastors reading this will find many reasons to disagree with me. The small church pastors that want to be big churches will find ways to believe it can all work with a larger congregation. Small groups, care groups, intentional discipleship groups, or whatever you call them, will be the suggested answer to the problems associated with large numbers. But I have comfortably come to the place where I think the ideal is found in small local churches that have a desire to birth more small churches if they grow numerically. Not satellite churches or multiple-site campus churches, but local gatherings of people centred around the unique local presence of Jesus in their context. I would like to believe that all we have discussed so far could be positively experienced in a large church, and it perhaps can, but not without more difficulty than in a small church. I openly confess that I am not sure how any of this can be experienced with success in a large church compared to a small church.

A good friend of mine who pastors a large church and completely disagrees with me on this issue once set me up in the best way possible to throw a great one-liner back at him. When our church plant was just getting going he made the comment to me that, "The hardest part will be getting over 200 people; it's like a speed bump that you just need to drive over." I responded, "I think that speed bump is Jesus and he's holding a stop sign saying, 'Don't do it!'" We laughed. And he still disagrees with me. But as I observe how the content of dialogue changes at leadership levels in larger churches, and how the programs and disciplines have to be constantly tweaked to accommodate numerical growth, I think we move further away from the ideal. Church is often still good, still transformative, and certainly still doing kingdom work, but further from the simple beauty of experiencing Jesus as our pastor through these methods. Simply put, it is just harder to remain close to the ideal the larger a church grows numerically. I believe more small churches living this way in an area will have greater effect on a surrounding community for the kingdom than will one large church.

Having said that, I hope that we can continue our conversation even if you disagree. My point is not that small churches are more appropriate, my point is that consensus is the ideal and is possible. Pursue that. I think we can all agree that no matter the size of our church or what our growth objectives are, our highest pursuit is Jesus.

I will finish this chapter with a story of non-consensus that led to consensus.

Our church was discerning whether or not we would donate funds to a local community project. We have a Community Involvement Fund to which people can give and through which we can come alongside projects within our surrounding community. This particular project centered around refurbishing a local historical landmark that was in dire need of repair. We commissioned some of our people to go to the site and pray about the idea. We conducted some casual interviews with residents in the community about what the landmark meant to them. We discussed the amount of money we would potentially contribute (it was not much in the grand scheme of what the project would entail, but it was something). Then during one of our regular Sunday gatherings we entered into a time of discernment using our model. We went through the entire process. Everyone shared their feelings, we took time to practice listening prayer, we discussed, and then went to a time of asking what everyone was sensing for where the Spirit was leading us. Would we have consensus? Everyone was on board with making the donation, except one person. They did not feel at peace about the decision. When asked if it was necessary for them to bring the decision to a full stop and say "no," they did just that. They could not stand aside; they had to say "stop." I give this person an immense amount of credit for doing so. It takes bravery to singularly take a strong stance. And as our process does not work on majority rules, we admitted we did not have consensus and that we would not contribute funds at that time but instead continue the process of discernment and research.

Part of this person's hesitations were around the charitable legalities of contributing our church funds to such a project. While at the time we all felt like we were not doing anything wrong but acting with wisdom and certainly following the law, we honoured our process and in turn, I believe, honoured the presence of Jesus in the room. We ended up putting more time into researching this person's concerns and finding out that while we were not doing anything wrong, we could do it better. The process led us to work with the Canadian Revenue Agency to craft new understandings for how a church like ours could appropriately finance contributions to community-endorsed projects. The understanding we came to has helped more churches with the same desire to work within their local communities to support projects. It turned out to be a huge win. If we had gone to a vote with the majority winning the day, we would have missed out on what became a great opportunity. Consensus does not promise speed and it does not promise always getting it right,

but I do believe it creates more space for Jesus to do good things in our midst.

6

New Models for Leadership

There are many theories out there regarding the best practices for leadership groups. In the church, every tradition, denomination, and local gathering has its own unique nuances, procedures, policies, and theological understanding of how leaders should and can lead. The spectrum ranges from entirely congregational to entirely hierarchical, but even when traditions share agreement on a particular style, leaders still shape their own language and titles. Leadership groups have specific names and functions, there are all sorts of different committees with different responsibilities that make up different teeth on the governance gears. All that to say, critiquing every denomination's governance model would be impossible in this space, and likely unhelpful. What I hope is to at least present an overarching framework — a guiding value — for an ethos of leadership in the local church. Hopefully, no matter the model in which you must abide according to your church tradition, this framework can influence *how* you make it work.

There is likely room to tweak it to align with your respective rules. I will also stick to a local setting, though certainly much could be said in regard to how our denominations apply governance models when everyone is in the room for decision-making time.

As I have said, I grew up in the Evangelical church. When I started to think about becoming a pastor, sometime in the late 90s, I began to pay attention to the popular trends and topics dominating the bookshelves of pastors and the conferences which they attended. Without doubt, the topic on everyone's radar was leadership. Churches like Saddleback in California and Willow Creek in the suburbs of Chicago were churning out materials and conferences. John Maxwell's *The 21 Irrefutable Laws of Leadership* was a must-read (it is currently in its 10th edition). And the list goes on.

Everyone wanted to be a great leader. If it was not explicitly said by the best speakers of the day, it was certainly implied, that *everything* hinged on good leadership. Churches would live and die, succeed or fail, be effective or useless, dependent on those who led them.

When I began my theological education in 1999 we had classes dedicated to leadership; we read all the books; we evaluated different leaders and we attempted to learn from the best. Classes that were not explicitly about leadership were shaped to view their topics through the surge of importance regarding leadership. Counselling became about leadership. Theology become about leadership. Biblical studies became about leadership. I remember believing that if I could effectively mimic the systems, disciplines, and cultures of great church leaders that were set before me, that I, too, could have a large ministry that affected positive change in the world and in people's lives. Interestingly, I do not remember ever having a pastor of a small church set before me as an affirming example of leadership. Be a great leader and have a great (big) church: it seemed to be that simple.

Even the way Jesus' ministry was explained encouraged me to see that he, too, must have read all the best leadership books. Jesus was obviously taking his cues from reading *The Maxwell Leadership Bible*. Emulating Jesus, which always sounds like a great idea, was just another way of becoming a great leader who would in turn have a great church.

Leadership. Nothing mattered more.

However, through all of those classes, books, and conferences, I felt tensions — things that did not settle well in my spirit. The most problematic tension was that I knew I did not measure up to these examples of leadership. I could not do what they did. I attended those conferences and for every part of me that felt encouraged and energized to *go get 'em* upon leaving, there were equal parts that wrestled with my own depravity and failings. The task of being that sort of leader felt impossible and incredibly daunting. It felt like so much rested on my ability to get it right. I had to make the best decisions. I had to create the best structures. I had to lead everyone to the promised land. I had to have all the answers. It was a weird mix of feeling completely inadequate and yet trying to tell myself that *I could* be all of those things to everyone. After all, these guys were doing it. It was all a bit terrifying. Perhaps most frightening was that, at least for me, the pursuit to becoming a good leader had something about it that lent itself to also pursuing power and fame. Certainly that was not the intent of all the teaching, but it was an outcome translated in my mind, nonetheless.

Another one of the tensions that I felt was that it all smelled a little too much like corporate America. The structures, the principals, the processes, the culture: in moments it felt like I was being taught to run a multinational corporation rather than the Spirit-infused Church of Jesus Christ. It did not sit right, but I did not know how to articulate my critique. The church was learning from corporate America, and although that felt weird to me, it was hard to argue with the "success" of many churches that were adopting those principals and leadership models.

I want to be clear that I sensed in many of the women and (mostly) men a sincere desire to pursue God and his kingdom. These men and women loved the church; they wanted what was best for her. They wanted to see God's kingdom on earth as it is in Heaven. But I could not shake the tensions. They ate at me.

So . . . you are expecting me to say that it was all wrong — that all those books, conferences, and classes missed the point. Not so, actually. I am thankful for so much of what I learned and continue to learn from the men and women who have spent countless hours researching, teaching, and living out many of these beliefs, theories, and values. Despite my own failings, misinterpretations, and mistakes, I believe I am a better leader because of what I was taught and the ideas presented to me upon which I was able to reflect. I do, actually, believe that many things, for better or worse, depend on leadership. Churches will live and die, succeed or fail, be effective or useless, dependent on leadership.

But I wonder if we missed something important?
Or at least, did I?

Everything does rise and fall on leadership, but whose leadership? Mine? Well, sort of. If I am to lead well, then I need to point people to the real leader. If I am to participate in good process, structures, and decision-making, then I need to do my part to direct everyone's gaze at the one who can show us the most appropriate processes, structures, and decisions for us in our time and place. If we are to have a church that is infused with the Spirit and power of God, then I need to help shape an environment where God can demonstrate those things. I am more convinced than ever that leadership matters, but it is Jesus who must be given a place to be the functional leader in our churches. My leadership matters, but it matters in so much as I point to Jesus as our church's pastor. It is about me, but not in the way that many of us have been led to believe.

I mentioned that the thought of having to measure up to the leadership gurus presented to me was terribly overwhelming and daunting. It still is. It could be suggested that what I am about to propose is merely my attempt at dealing with my own inadequacies and poor self-esteem on this matter. I have had some people critique the forthcoming model by suggesting I need only have more confidence and then I would not need a model like this. In essence they are suggesting that I am shirking my responsibility to lead — giving it away because I am too scared to "make the big decisions" or "have the buck stop with me." In a way I agree with that critique. I am scared of all those things, but perhaps in a way different from what is being suggested. I am scared at the heart level of it all. I am scared because I know my own confidence level can be *too high* — I can want the buck to stop with me *too much*. The appeal of ruling my own kingdom is *too real*. We can all get a little bit like King David and his need to "count the troops" in 2 Samuel 24. I can forget whose kingdom this is. In Evangelical land, the cult of the celebrity pastor can be blamed for this, but that is too abstract. The truth is that the celebrity pastor culture only comes about because we pastors allow it, even foster and celebrate it. On paper all of us would agree that the church — our local church — is not ours at all; she is God's church. The people are God's. The future of our church is in God's hands. But the temptation to become the reason for success (never failure, of course) creeps in and before we know it, we have allowed a system to be built around us that points everything to us. The celebrity pastor often exists because a pastor loves the spotlight. We can love — crave — having the buck stop on our desk. What I am about to propose can safeguard us from becoming our own worst enemy. However, that is only a wonderful bonus to what is really the point of this.

What I am about to suggest *does* require leadership. It requires good leadership. It is not a shirking of responsibility; in fact, it is the greatest of all our responsibilities as a church leader. It is about creating models that intentionally focus people on Jesus, not us, and not even on the model itself.

I was having a coffee one day with my friend Michael Knowles, my professor from seminary. Our meeting together on that occasion was during the early days of our church plant. It was just before I hit the wall, before my wife's cancer diagnosis and everything else that fell apart. I remember telling him I was beginning to feel like I was losing control.

A couple of weeks earlier, our church had held its first service. Up until that point we had been meeting in smaller groups without weekly consistency. This was our first time together doing what could be considered a traditional Sunday service. Except it was on a Monday night and it was in a bar. But besides that, it was a fairly cookie-cutter church service: some music, preaching, communion, announcements, prayer, Scripture reading...all the typical components. The thing was, except for the singing, I led all of it. I welcomed people, I preached, I did it all. Now, this is not about whether that was the right or wrong thing to do. This is not about how you should or should not lead a church service. But for me, on that night, it completely exhausted me in a way no church service had ever done before. I went into it with a belief that somehow I needed to carry this thing we had started. I had incredibly high expectations of myself that night, and deep within I wanted to believe that as soon as I said, "You're dismissed," everyone would run into the streets evangelizing to the world and welcoming newcomers into the fullness of God's kingdom. None of that happened, of course. I went home deflated and depressed. Nothing had gone wrong; no one had complained about anything — just the opposite, in fact.

By all accounts it was a great night.
But not for me.

I told Michael about this experience. Even though he is an ordained Anglican Priest and the professor of preaching at a Baptist seminary, Michael is deeply charismatic. Sitting together, I experienced one of those instances where someone with that depth of gifting reads into your situation and you immediately sense in your gut that it is actually the Spirit using them to speak truth and to bring illumination. Michael encouraged me; he affirmed I was a great leader. He reminded me of others who had experienced and said the same thing about me. He spoke back to me comments that I had at one point said to him as a way of reminding me that I knew what I was doing. But after this time of encouragement, he took me to the next place I needed to go. I needed that encouragement, that I was and needed to be a good leader — yes, all the leadership stuff I had been taught and experienced mattered. *But*, it all only mattered in as much as I could realize that it was not about me. It was not that I could not or should not ever be up in front of people taking responsibility, and not that I should not lead, and lead well. But in all that I did as a leader, it had to *be about Jesus*. It was the heart of the matter that needed to change. Little did I know that I was entering into a time in my life where tears in coffee shops would become a common occurrence. I wanted everyone to know that I could lead. I wanted them to know that I could lead us to the promised land — that I could shoulder the responsibility and get us to where God wanted us. But in the midst of leading I forgot who really takes his people to the promised land.

Moses is the most revered leader in Jewish history. No one led better than him. But it was his unwillingness to lead without God that has encouraged and challenged me the most as I think about his make-up as a leader. Too often we glorify the "heroes of the faith" for their character qualities and capabilities, when what I actually find to be most challenging and comforting is understanding and relating to their incredible weakness and human frailty. It is in their mess, doubt, and struggle that I see the power and strength of a faithful and loving God. He is, of course, the real hero.

Immediately following the debacle of the golden calf, God has a chat with Moses. At this point, after witnessing the people completely come off the rails, Moses is likely seriously questioning his capacity to lead. There is a sense in which I see Moses standing in front of the proverbial wall, feeling like there is no way forward or around it. I sense his dawning realization that he will not be able to get the job done; there will be no promised land. Frankly, you get the sense that God is almost at the same place. But then there is this beautiful conversation between the two in Exodus:

> *The Lord said to Moses, "Go and leave this place, you and the people whom you brought up out of the land of Egypt. Go to the land I promised to Abraham, Isaac, and Jacob when I said, 'I'll give it to your descendants.' I'll send a messenger before you. I'll drive out the Canaanites, the Amorites, the Hittites, the Perizzites, the Hivites, and the Jebusites. Go to*

this land full of milk and honey. But I won't go up with you because I would end up destroying you along the way since you are a stubborn people."

Exodus 33:1-3

Moses said to the Lord, "Look, you've been telling me, 'Lead these people forward.' But you haven't told me whom you will send with me. Yet you've assured me, 'I know you by name and think highly of you.' Now if you do think highly of me, show me your ways so that I may know you and so that you may really approve of me. Remember too that this nation is your people."

The Lord replied, "I'll go myself, and I'll help you."

Moses replied, "If you won't go yourself, don't make us leave here. Because how will anyone know that we have your special approval, both I and your people, unless you go with us? Only that distinguishes us, me and your people, from every other people on the earth."

The Lord said to Moses, "I'll do exactly what you've asked because you have my special approval, and I know you by name."

Moses said, "Please show me your glorious presence."

Exodus 33:12-18

And then a few verses later in Exodus 34 we read that God indeed does show his presence to Moses.

> *The Lord passed in front of him and proclaimed:*
> *"The Lord! The Lord!*
> *a God who is compassionate and merciful,*
> *very patient,*
> *full of great loyalty and faithfulness,*
> *showing great loyalty to a thousand generations,*
> *forgiving every kind of sin and rebellion,*
> *yet by no means clearing the guilty,*
> *punishing for their parents' sins*
> *their children and their grandchildren,*
> *as well as the third and the fourth generation."*

Exodus 34:6-7

This encounter did not tell Moses to stop being a leader. It did not allow Moses to shirk his responsibility as a leader. As I said, Moses is remembered as a great leader. He went on to do some remarkable things. But this exposes the heart of a true leader of God's people. We will not lead — we *cannot* lead — if God does not come with us. His presence is all we must desire. His presence with us and for us, leading us and constantly demonstrating his compassion, mercy, patience, steadfast love, faithfulness, and forgiveness must be the focal point of our leadership. We must lead well, with wisdom, discernment, courage, and love, but all that we do must point to the one who is leading us all. Our models and methods must draw people into this awareness of God's presence and his leadership.

My leadership team conducts an evaluation of me once every two years. I ask them to perform this and they do a great job of it. An aspect of the evaluation is to survey a few people from the church with a selection of questions that have to do with my service and leadership. There is one question asked that I care about the most. Every question is important, but this question is where, when presented with the results, my eyes first go. The question is this: "How well does Aaron consistently point the congregation toward the leadership of Jesus?" It is rated from 1 to 5. In my opinion, anything less than a 5 means I have work to do. The apostle Paul knew this well: I must decrease so Jesus can increase. If I trust Jesus as the Good Shepherd, then I must point to him as our leader and pastor. I want people to say that their pastor is Jesus, not Aaron. I want people to see past me right to the Father.

If leadership classes and books have taught me anything, it is that values and preferred-futures must first be lived out at the leadership level. Leadership needs to be an example. This means our models of governance need to be reimagined. The guiding value of pointing to Jesus through our leadership must be reflected in the nuts and bolts of how we lead. Therefore, I submit to you what we do at our church. Now, everyone says this when they present their own church's ideas, and I will say the same thing: our model is not perfect. I mean that. It is a work in progress. We have been using it for several years and we continue to tweak it. But I hope it at least gets the wheels turning.

This is our model:

Leadership Team Guiding Value:

Our Leadership Team (LT) will make decisions and provide direction, but it will do so in a way that seeks to value the ultimate leading of the Spirit, relationships within the LT and larger church community, an ethos of mutual submission, and the Kingdom values on which the church community is built.

Practically speaking:

The LT will function as a mutually submitting table of equals with Jesus as the Lead Pastor. The minister's job is to resource the LT's discussions, present ideas, and continually point the discussion towards Jesus and the mission to which Jesus has called the church and the minister. The minister will be expected to live in obedience to the calling and vision that Jesus has placed in his/her heart. The minister is a catalyst, but will rely on the LT to lead as a group.

The primary concerns of the LT are to listen to Jesus and the church community, reflect Kingdom values amongst each other, and empower and encourage the church community by providing direction and decision-making. Specifically, the LT will not make decisions based on majority voting; rather, the LT will prayerfully await confirmation on decisions from the voice of Jesus and move forward only with consensus.

The LT will operate with the belief that the Spirit can and will lead to truth, consensus, and a process for moving forward. This will happen through prayerful discernment, discussion, debate, Scripture-searching, and consultation with the Tradition. This belief, however, does not dismiss the possibility that risks and experiments may fail. However, this belief does mean that even in the failures, the "failed" processes and relationships within the LT and church are still of value and in the midst of being sanctified.

The LT will prayerfully discuss pertinent big-picture issues related to the church's guiding values. When the LT comes to Spirit-led consensus on issues, it may present the issues to the church for discussion and critique. This is not permission-seeking, but rather an opportunity for continued discernment of the Spirit's leading. If there is pushback from the church, the LT will assume that they did not explain things properly, missed something, or need to see the pushback as a caution or "no" from the Spirit. In this case, the LT will re-discuss the issue and either return to the church with a reconstructed presentation or will leave the discussion for a later date or altogether. If the response to the issue is positive, the LT will take appropriate action. These gatherings will not include voting; rather, they will be a structured discussion (see the previously discussed discernment process in chapter four).

Those a part of the church community who are not on the LT should know and feel that their voice is still important. The LT will work diligently to ensure this.

Further, the LT will not become the visual demonstration of everything done for and in the church. For example, children, youth, teaching, hospitality, other leadership responsibilities, and serving in whatever capacity are all still areas in which those not a part of the LT can and should be involved.

The LT will meet regularly and will provide timely updates to the church community.

Something we need to explicitly add to this document, which we have always practiced, is the need for a table, good food, and good drinks. I sincerely believe that much of how we practice our leadership values is made possible because we eat together. I could never go back to any sort of church board meeting that did not include beginning with simply being friends around food and drink in someone's home. It is within that environment that I believe we create the best space for our work as leaders.

In terms of praxis, we make this value come alive by presenting an idea, talking, and then intentionally leaving space for listening prayer, discernment, and quiet. Sometimes we are able to just make a decision. God has, after all, given us brains and we are each hopefully growing in maturity and wisdom each day. Sometimes a decision can be made as easily as everyone looking at each other and saying, "Yep." Other times you get a sense, if you have intentionally shaped an atmosphere of listening and openness to the Spirit, that a decision requires some discernment. As we pay attention to the prompts in our head, heart, and gut, sometimes someone, or everyone, will say we need to take some time on a decision. In those spaces I have had to learn how to honour introverts and extroverts. I have had to learn how to honour those who need time to listen to Jesus and contemplate. I have had to learn how to care more about the process than the outcome. A couple of chapters ago I mentioned that speed is not the goal in most of these practices, and that is true again here. The most important thing is meeting with Jesus and caring for each other around the table. Jesus' ministry to us and our ministry to each other is what really breathes these values into life.

Perhaps all of this prompts more questions than answers; perhaps you already use something far better. But I hope the heartbeat of this discussion at least prompts some good reflection. Like I said, you will no doubt have models that are a part of your tradition's mandated way of leading and decision-making. There may be steps you take in order to comply with what is expected of you by your denomination. But hopefully this discussion can help you think about how you nuance those expectations, how you bring the value of Jesus as the lead pastor to the table,

and how you go about leading in a way that always points people to Jesus.

New Expectations

7

The Table

I refer to myself as a deprived sacramentalist. In this journey of trying to figure out ways to make tangible the presence of Jesus in my life and church, I have had to deal with this.

Growing up in a Christian & Missionary Alliance Church, participating in communion was a monthly occurrence. It was served on the last Sunday of the month with little individual plastic cups of grape juice and perfectly square-cut pieces of *delicious* unhealthy white bread. Unfortunately, it was almost always held at the end of the Sunday morning service, which, as a kid, immediately put communion in a negative light. The regular service never seemed to get any shorter on those Sundays, so communion always made the service longer. I am sure that sometimes communion was intentionally connected to what had just happened in the service, but I do not remember it that way. My recollection is that most of the time it was more of an addendum. It was important; I knew that. But it stood on its own without much connection to the rest of our life together as a church family.

Its meaning in my mind was quite simple. We needed to remember that Jesus died for us; it was a time to confess our sin before we took the bread and juice. It was really slow, solemn, quiet, retrospective, and carried out with military-like pageantry. Keep in mind that those observations are through the eyes of a young kid, and few children enjoy slow, solemn, quiet, and retrospective activities. More importantly, I remember that there was never mention made of anything mysterious happening in the activity. If anything, that sort of thing was quietly dismissed. After all, while evangelicals may not know exactly what it means to be evangelical, we know we are not Catholic. I have no doubt this differentiation influenced the simplicity of communion in my church. Communion was a symbol, or, in our Christian & Missionary Alliance language, an ordinance: an outward symbol of an internal understanding of Jesus death and resurrection. My understanding of communion was to bring to light my sin and then to ask Jesus to forgive me so I could quickly digest the bread and juice before accidentally or intentionally sinning again. Very little *happened* at the communion table

As I became older my understanding of communion changed. It broadened along with my own spiritual maturity, but it remained quite logical, simple, and routine. It was still most often presented as ritual, symbol, and an important act of obedience, all of which are appropriate descriptors, but it was about intellectual assent versus any sort of transformational experience or discovery.

Theologically speaking, Jesus was there in some capacity (as he always is). Experientially, for me, he was not.

How did my tradition of the faith simplify the Lord's Supper to this level? Since the beginning of the church, the majority of Christians and traditions around the world have viewed and experienced The Table in a profound way. It has been and is central to the gathered experience of followers of Jesus. What is going on for them in that moment? What was I missing? What are we missing if our understanding is only as deep as mine was at a young age? My tradition desired to experience and know Jesus in a hands-on sort of way. For example, we believe wholeheartedly in the laying on of hands for blessing, commissioning, and healing, so why not fully embrace a religious practice like communion that likewise embraces that perspective and expectation?

It was during a denominational event years ago that one of our pastors spoke about his own journey to discovering the importance and experience of The Table. As I listened to him something in my heart came alive as I deeply resonated with both his experiences within our shared denominational history and his coming to a new paradigm of communion. Rev. Brian Buhler used the Emmaus road text and it forever changed my understanding. What I present now began with what Brian shared that day.

> *On that same day, two disciples were traveling to a village called Emmaus, about seven miles from Jerusalem. They were talking to each other about everything that had happened. While they were discussing these things, Jesus himself arrived and joined them on their journey. They were*

prevented from recognizing him.

He said to them, "What are you talking about as you walk along?" They stopped, their faces downcast.

The one named Cleopas replied, "Are you the only visitor to Jerusalem who is unaware of the things that have taken place there over the last few days?"

He said to them, "What things?"

They said to him, "The things about Jesus of Nazareth. Because of his powerful deeds and words, he was recognized by God and all the people as a prophet. But our chief priests and our leaders handed him over to be sentenced to death, and they crucified him. We had hoped he was the one who would redeem Israel. All these things happened three days ago. But there's more: Some women from our group have left us stunned. They went to the tomb early this morning and didn't find his body. They came to us saying that they had even seen a vision of angels who told them he is alive. Some of those who were with us went to the tomb and found things just as the women said. They didn't see him."

Then Jesus said to them, "You foolish people! Your dull minds keep you from believing all that the prophets talked about. Wasn't it necessary for the Christ to suffer these things and then enter into his glory?" Then he interpreted for them the things written about himself in all the scriptures, starting with Moses and going through all the Prophets.

151

When they came to Emmaus, he acted as if he was going on ahead. But they urged him, saying, "Stay with us. It's nearly evening, and the day is almost over." So he went in to stay with them. After he took his seat at the table with them, he took the bread, blessed and broke it, and gave it to them. Their eyes were opened and they recognized him, but he disappeared from their sight. They said to each other, "Weren't our hearts on fire when he spoke to us along the road and when he explained the scriptures for us?"

They got up right then and returned to Jerusalem. They found the eleven and their companions gathered together. They were saying to each other, "The Lord really has risen! He appeared to Simon!" Then the two disciples described what had happened along the road and how Jesus was made known to them as he broke the bread.

Luke 24:13-35

This story tells us that Jesus was with the disciples on the road, but that the disciples did not recognize him. How can that be? Surely he must have been wearing his white robe and blue sash? Were his long flowing European locks of hair not waving softly in the breeze? Somehow, in a remarkably mysterious way, the disciples were blinded to the physical identity of Jesus. He was there, but they could not see him. He was speaking to them, but they could not tell it was his voice. At this point all we can do is assume one thing: Jesus did not want them to see and hear him as they had prior to his crucifixion.

It seems that in Luke 24 the church is being prepared for the new way of interacting with the resurrected Jesus. The two travellers are us. We are people who will need to know, see, and experience Jesus without seeing and experiencing him in his fleshly form. The entirety of what I have suggested so far in this book is moot if we cannot do this. We need a unique means of meeting with Jesus and having our eyes opened to his presence, despite the fact that his physical heart-pumping body is ascended to the Father.

Sacrament can be a scary word for Protestants. It sounds too Catholic. Try for a moment to start from scratch with this word. The definition is simply how, in a particular place, action, or time, people can experience the grace and love of God. A sacrament is a place or time in which our good and gracious God is uniquely worshipped, acknowledged, discovered, or experienced. Generally speaking, then, all of time and space could be considered a sacrament. And perhaps that is the way it ought to be. But what we know from our human experience is that there are particular times we intentionally focus on and expect to interact with God. We build these moments into our lives as rhythms. This is religion at its best. They are times that are somehow more than simple routine, though religious routine is often the way we purposefully ensure we set aside time to do these things. More than routine, they are intentionally unique moments. They are unique in that the interaction is between us and God, but God does the work in that time. In sacrament, we acknowledge God is present therein — it is a special moment where the space between the now and the coming Kingdom is thin — and we make ourselves available to God's presence working and speaking. We faithfully set aside the time or engage in the action, and God does his transformational thing in the midst of it.

The Emmaus Road story goes a long way in teaching us about sacrament.

The first sacrament within this text is biblical preaching. The disciples do not know it is Jesus, but his preaching has changed and challenges them. In that space and time, something uniquely divine has happened. Jesus' words from the Scriptures "burned in their hearts." As Evangelicals we are all over this sacrament. It is our hallmark. For the most part we do it pretty well. The Spirit which inspired the words of Scripture continues to use those words today to shape and change us and to reveal God's story of redemption and hope. Preaching is a way we experience God's love and grace. It is a sacrament.

But the story of Emmaus also talks about a second sacrament: The Lord's Supper, Communion, The Eucharist. While hearts burned after the preaching, eyes were only opened after the breaking of the bread. This is where we start to get nervous in our tradition. Is it reformation baggage?[1] Is it fear of mystery to our modern-shaped minds and churches? Whatever it is, I am suggesting we need to set those fears aside, to educate our Reformation ignorance, and try to interact with and engage in this ancient act with fresh eyes.

The great Italian painter, Caravaggio, has a painting which brilliantly depicts this moment.

---

1 As mentioned before, I suggest checking out D.H. Williams' book, *Retrieving the Tradition and Renewing Evangelicalism: A Primer for Suspicious Protestants*.

In Caravaggio's painting[2] an unfamiliar guest becomes a very familiar host. Suddenly, the stranger is no longer merely intriguing, but one who can preach with power — it is the Saviour himself in their midst and the disciples are blown away. As they grip the table in shock and exclaim with hand gestures, eyes are opened to the presence of Jesus. When? Only after the bread has been broken. Their eyes are opened to the love and grace of God, manifested in the presence of Jesus, during communion.

It is much more than a ritual, a solemn observance, an ordinance, or a place to confess our sins: communion is where we encounter the risen Jesus in a unique way. It is the centrepiece of our gathering together as followers of Jesus. Everything

---

[2] *Supper at Emmaus by Caravaggio.* 1606. Currently located in the Pinacoteca di Brera, Milan.

before Eucharist is foreplay. If that sounds a bit sexual, it should, because intimacy at its deepest level is found in Communion.

Speaking of sex, I have heard it said that practicing Eucharist every week instead of once a month diminishes the specialness or uniqueness of the event. It is said that if we do it too much it loses its evocative power and beauty. I suppose there could be something to this, but only if you choose to believe that the cup and bread are only a cup and bread. If in the bread and cup there is the presence of Jesus in some unique way, then this is about experiencing intimacy with someone who we love more than any other. To those who suggest that too much Eucharist is a bad thing, I ask them whether they would tell a married couple, deeply in love with each other, to keep the sex to a minimum? I doubt it. At The Table is where we become intimate with Jesus, and it ought to happen regularly.

Jesus chose to vanish not after the sermon was done but after the bread was handed out and in their hands. With hearts burning from the living Scriptures, hands full of bread, and eyes opened to see Jesus in their midst and to know his presence, he can depart and set his people loose. To keep the sexual intimacy analogy going, it is in the intimate moment between us and Jesus at The Table that procreation takes place: mission is birthed. Our churches need a worship encounter with God that will sustain and empower them to do their thing. If all we have is good Biblical teaching, we do not have enough. There is power, grace, and presence in the Lord's Table because it was ordained by Jesus to empower us to be his church – the very body of Christ to the world. Without the sort of intimacy encountered at The Table, the church will not have what it takes to keep building on its relationship with Jesus, and to parent and nurture its offspring.

Have you been sacramentally deprived? Have you kept your church from meeting with Jesus in this way? Are you a sacramental observer, but you do not think anything actually happens in the sacraments? Can you submit your practice of The Table to Jesus and create space for him to minister? I suggest that Evangelicals do this very well in some forms of worship. Through music, Evangelicals will often enter into an expectation for Jesus to meet with them, to hear from him, and to sense his loving arms. Can we approach the Table with the same expectation? Can we set aside that time as a unique place for Jesus to minister? Is there a better time and place to engage in prayer for the sick and hurting? Is there a better place to celebrate and give thanks? Is there a better place from which to move into mission? I think not. If we want to have Jesus pastor us, if as pastors we want to intentionally create space to get out of the way and allow Jesus to minister to his people, we must embrace this tradition of the church that, sadly, has too often been glossed over by Evangelicals.

John Wesley wrote in Hymn 71, "The sign transmits the signified." Wesley, along with his brother Charles, wrote 166 real-presence Eucharistic songs and hymns. They are a treasure trove of great theology. For example:

> *Jesus, at whose supreme command*
> *We thus approach to God,*
> *Before us in Thy vesture stand,*

Thy vesture dipp'd in blood.
Obedient to Thy gracious word,
We break the hallow'd bread,
Commemorate Thee, our dying Lord,
And trust on Thee to feed.
Now, Saviour, now Thyself reveal,
And make Thy nature known;
Affix the sacramental seal,
And stamp us for Thine own.
The tokens of Thy dying love
O let us all receive
And feel the quickening Spirit move,
And sensibly believe.
The cup of blessing, blest by Thee,
Let it Thy blood impart.
The bread Thy mystic body be,
And cheer each languid heart.
The grace which sure salvation brings
Let us herewith receive;
Satiate the hungry with good things,
The hidden manna give.

> Hymns on the Lord's Supper, Hymn 30,
> in Rattenbury, 1996: 168

The heavenly ordinances shine,
And speak their origin Divine.

> Hymns on the Lord's Supper, Hymn 62,
> in Rattenbury, 1996: 176.

Strikingly, none of them made it into the original hymnbook of my childhood C&MA tradition, which is no doubt a reflection of the "ordinance" theology in which I was raised. But I do not want to throw my tradition under the bus. Somewhere along the line my tradition forgot where she came from in this regard. The founder of my tradition, Albert Benjamin Simpson, discussed his position:

> *Roman Catholics teach that in the Lord's Supper the bread and wine are converted into the actual flesh of Christ (but) it would do us no good if we could actually eat the flesh of Christ; it would be profane cannibalism. But if we can receive that which lies back of His flesh, His vital strength into our being, that is all we need. And that is the real substance of the resurrection body. He is the embodiment of life and power, and by the Holy Spirit He imparts to us that life and power as we worthily receive the sacrament and discern Him in it.[3]*

Okay, so Simpson had some Roman Catholic issues he needed to work through, but he did not shy away from talking about the unique time of ministry and power that takes place in the bread and wine.

The Apostle Paul calls the Lord's Supper participation in the blood and body of Christ. Jesus is there with us in the breaking of the bread by some mystery. Real presence. And where Jesus is, so too is transformation. And if this mystery bothers you, may I remind you that Jesus rose from the dead. If that mystery is okay

---

[3] A.B. Simpson in *Lord for the Body. Tracts for the Times: Divine Healing Series.* c.1900.

with you but this one is not, than I am not sure I can help you.

———

During the height of my anxiety and fear surrounding Shalene's cancer and my son's seizures, I was attending a weekly program at a nearby church with a focus on allowing Jesus to minister into our broken places. The program had been incredibly helpful in teaching me about listening prayer and helping me to learn to see Jesus in all the places of my life.

The final week of the program began with teaching and worship, and then we were going to conclude our time together with communion. For me it was another day of dark depression, fear, and anxiety. I could barely keep still in my seat as my mind raced between doubt and desperation. Even in that building surrounded by people who cared for me and had been walking with me through those dark times, my mind quickly fell into darkness, thoughts of suicide, and feelings of complete despair.

I remember sitting in my row and having it out with Jesus. I would often scream inside my head, "Are you real? Will you save me from this?" I could see the bread and cup sitting on the table in front of all of us and I was talking to it hoping that Jesus would hear me. "Will you meet me there, Jesus? Because I need you." I was so desperate for it all to be real.

As I stood up and went forward to take the bread and the cup, I felt nervous, like I was stepping into someone's home, not knowing if they were there or if the place was abandoned and empty. I was looking for someone, but was not sure they were real. I was hoping to see someone, but I was not sure they could see me. I ripped a chunk of bread from the loaf and ate it. I lifted the cup and drank. And what happened to me, as never had before, was a rush of peace that coursed through me with a bizarre and strangely calming intensity. If that does not make sense, I trust you can appreciate how hard it is to put words to the presence of Jesus. He was there in that moment. He ministered to me in a unique way at the Table with overcoming peace. I did not get answers. I did not suddenly have the ability to make sense of all my troubles. But I knew he was there with me.

A quote, often attributed to John Calvin, states, "[A] trifle mysterious, that the Eucharist is a feast of both absence and presence, and so it always is in the business of faith."

For those who go looking, he is there at the Table. For 2000 years the vast majority of Christians around the world have known this to be true about The Eucharist. He is there. We set aside time to gather as the church to be led and ministered to by the presence of Jesus. It is all foreplay for what happens at The Table.

The Lord's Supper is where intimacy is most revealed.

PRAYER

O God,
the risen Christ revealed himself to his disciples
in the breaking of bread.
Feed us with the bread of life
and break open our hearts,
that we may know him
not only in the good news of the scriptures,
but risen and in the midst of your pilgrim people. Amen.[4]

---

[4] Taken from the *Revised Common Lectionary*. Church Publications Inc, 2008.

8

A New Unity

Instead, by speaking the truth with love, let's grow in every way into Christ, who is the head. The whole body grows from him, as it is joined and held together by all the supporting ligaments. The body makes itself grow in that it builds itself up with love as each one does its part.

Ephesians 4:15-16

One of the first things I did when I began work on our new church was to track down every local minister in town. I had several reasons for doing this, but most importantly I knew that I wanted to work together with like-minded people. In my case, there was a functioning monthly gathering of these ministers so it was not overly difficult. You may have to work harder than I did. In our ministerial group we have Catholics, Presbyterians, Anglicans, Mainliners, Pentecostals, a couple flavours of Dutch Reformed,

Baptist, and me, from the Christian & Missionary Alliance. Needless to say, it is an eclectic group with many different theological positions. We each do church differently. And like any group, each of us connect more easily with some than others simply based on personality types, personal interests, hobbies, stage of life, and the like. This is to be expected. Despite all of our differences, though, we are united by a common person: Jesus. It sounds so simplistic, but this centering figure enables something beautiful to take place. We are all on the same team. And though our methods might be different, we have a common desire to see the kingdom of God come on earth as it is in Heaven. Again, I know this sounds simplistic. But the simplicity of a unity found in Jesus is really all you need to move forward and to pursue the kingdom. If this common belief worked for prostitutes, Roman soldiers, and other lowly characters, certainly it can work for such upstanding people as clergy. (Please note the sarcasm.)

Despite the incredible differences between the nuts and bolts of how we do church on a weekly basis, these ministers have become some of my greatest allies in our community. Throughout the year we combine our congregations for different events and times of worship. This requires some creativity because of the different views on some practices. However, we enjoy exposing our people to each other's unique practices and passions. It creates great conversations between the differing church institutions, and it builds relationships that in many cases have been broken by years of misinformed and, to be quite honest, ignorant opinions of each other. Actually, to put it bluntly, there is centuries of sin between Christians that has trickled down to us all. But the reconciliation Jesus enables is beautiful and powerful. Just a few weeks ago our church combined with three other churches to celebrate, pray, and commemorate the Week of Prayer for Christian Unity. We held the service at the Anglican Church, but each of us clergy, and our people, participated in different parts of the service. It was beautiful. To close the service each of us ministers stood in front of the altar and proclaimed the benediction.

Father Ian (Catholic): **May the Father, whose glory fills the heavens, cleanse you by his holiness and send you to proclaim his word. Amen.**

Me (Protestant): **May the Son, who has ascended to the heights, pour upon you the riches of his grace. Amen.**

Father Jim (Anglican): **May the Holy Spirit, the Comforter, equip you and strengthen you in your ministry. Amen.**

(All together): **And may the blessing of God Almighty, Father, Son and Holy Spirit, be upon you and remain with you always. Amen.**

Speaking of Father Ian, he has become a friend in spite of, and in many cases, because of our differences. We have known each other for several years and our lives are very different, both personally and vocationally. He is older than me, he is single, he has no kids, he lives in the same building as his church, and his life is incredibly busy with all the things that Catholic priests must do (it is a long list). The words "day off" are not a part of his vocabulary. His church is well established and it is a good size.

And yet our bond is real.

As I said, Father Ian's home is the local parish building. Upstairs above the offices are combined living quarters: his, the associate priest's, and those for occasional seminarians. They each have their own small living area with a large shared common room, kitchen, and dining area. It is all quite nice, but it is the common room that takes the cake. I call it "The George Clooney Room." Imagine a room where George Clooney would sit back and sip scotch while smoking a nice cigar. That is this room. It is home to the two best leather reclining chairs I have ever encountered and a couch that envelops you into its loving embrace. The room is painted in dark greys with dark hardwood floor planks. Fine art hangs on the walls and there are dark oak cabinets and shelves which are home to great books and fine bottles of various adult beverages. It is a sophisticated man cave. Fittingly, it was there where I was first introduced to great scotch.

With scotch in hand I have sat in that room and chatted for hours with Ian and the others who live and work there. We laugh at each other; we make sarcastic remarks about each other's practices and traditions, and we also have conversations about what makes our specific traditions and practices a part of the dynamic shaping of a person's faith and understanding of God and the Church. We share our frustrations with our traditions and we try to convince each other of the best of our traditions. We talk shop. But we also talk about our doubts, our unanswered prayers, our personal growing pains in the faith, and the trials of some of our parishioners. We are connected by deeply human things and deeply divine things.

It is in this relationship that I have experienced the reality of a good theology and practice of ecumenism. It is in this relationship that I have had confirmed the power of Jesus to unify those from different Christian traditions. The amount of times we have asked for forgiveness from the other because of our own tradition's ignorance and down-right sin towards the other has been countless. Jesus is there with us breathing to life reconciliation and common mission between his children, even if it is just two at a time.

We have preached from each other's pulpits (an incredible honour for a rebellious Protestant like me!). On one occasion I did a Q&A with him for our church during a Sunday gathering. I asked him what he noticed in terms of similarities and differences between our two traditions, both theological and regarding how we "do" church. He began by making this wonderful pronouncement: "We have so much in common because at a base level, we believe the story of Jesus and his presence with us is normative." We have what matters most in common.

For too long the pursuit of unity in the church has been confined to only our local church or within our particular denominations. Which, I admit, is sometimes enough of a challenge to occupy all our time. But I want to suggest that the heartbeat of Paul's hopeful challenge in Ephesians 4:1-6 is greater, larger, and far more encompassing than only being restricted to our local congregations. If Jesus is allowed to be the pastor and leader in our leadership and church, quite possibly unity is absolutely something to be realized *between* churches of different Christian traditions, not just inside our own church or our own tradition.

Immediately before Paul's call to unity we find his cosmic explanation regarding the movement of God's kingdom and his prayer for the church in Ephesus. This cosmic-sized "secret plan" of the power of Jesus' life, death, and resurrection is unleashed on the world through love and grace. In this monumental redemptive movement, all people, all nations, and all ethnicities are drawn together in Christ. It is nothing short of breathtaking. It brings together people from everywhere who no doubt have all manner of differences, and differences often create challenges. For this reason, Paul prays these words:

This is why I kneel before the Father. Every ethnic group in heaven or on earth is recognized by him. I ask that he will strengthen you in your inner selves from the riches of his glory through the Spirit. I ask that Christ will live in your hearts through faith. As a result of having strong roots in love, I ask that you'll have the power to grasp love's width and length, height and depth, together with all believers. I ask that you'll know the love of Christ that is beyond knowledge so that you will be filled entirely with the fullness of God.

Glory to God, who is able to do far beyond all that we could ask or imagine by his power at work within us; glory to him in the church and in Christ Jesus for all generations, forever and always. Amen.

Ephesians 3:14-21

Paul earnestly asks that Christ be vibrantly alive inside all believers, desiring that because of this they will each be able to grasp, and reflect in harmony with all believers, the incredible dynamic love of Jesus. It is quite the prayer request. But Paul knows this is necessary, because the next thing he talks about is unity in the faith.

Therefore, as a prisoner for the Lord, I encourage you to live as people worthy of the call you received from God. Conduct yourselves with all humility, gentleness, and patience. Accept each other with love, and make an effort to preserve the unity of the Spirit with the peace that ties you together. You are one body and one spirit, just as God also called you in one hope. There is one Lord, one faith, one baptism, and one God and Father of all, who is over all, through all, and in all.

Ephesians 4:1-6

We have to keep the preceding cosmic statements he made in mind. This cannot simply be limited to the life together of our local church, it must be about all Christian churches. If there is to be this sort of unity in the faith, then the indwelling of Jesus and an understanding of his incredible love must permeate the lives of all believers.

Two thousand years of church history has taught us that unity in the faith is not easy. Schism —a wide split between arguing parties — has been the church's trademark more than it has been reconciliation or consistent unity together. Catholic, Orthodox, Anglican, Lutheran, Baptist, Pentecostal, Protestant, Mainline: no one has been immune from schism. It is heartbreaking, I am sure, for the God who exists in perfect triune unity. It is why Paul's prayer for the believers in Ephesus, and for us, was so necessary and so audacious.

There was a time in the west during the reign of Christendom that the church could, to some extent, get away with the constant forming of new denominations. While schism is unhelpful and ultimately negative, it did not stop the church from remaining at the centre of culture. Without doubt these schisms had lasting negative effects on the following generations of the church, but for centuries the church remained dominant in its context. Those days are long gone. The church in the west cannot afford to allow schism to continue. Schism and division thwarts the mission of the church in our time and worse, it grieves the heart of God. At a time when we as the church have been moved to the margins of culture, we cannot afford infighting for the sake of a falsely perceived doctrinal purity that no one outside of our church walls cares about. I am not suggesting that working towards doctrinal purity is unnecessary or a negative pursuit, but the future must be in doing this *together* as Christian traditions and not in our silos.

Soon after Shalene was diagnosed with cancer, many of the ministers from other local churches in town consistently reminded me they were asking for Jesus to heal her. They were joining with us in our pain and fear. Pain and suffering can be a great unifier. Suffering is a place where our humanity connects one to another on a deep level. As Christians we can be united in our realtime struggle for faith in a world where darkness sometimes feels all-encompassing. I think if we are all honest with each other then we can admit we have our moments of doubt, moments of asking "Is this real?" and moments of panic thinking that we have given ourselves to something that seems to have let us down. Catholic, Anglican, Protestant: our faith is linked in a profound way by our pain, disappointment, yearning for more, our desire for healing, and our admission that we are a broken people who need a saviour. Many of our forebears in each of our traditions have stories and experiences of the dark nights of the soul — moments where the ache of longing for God to enter into their doubt and hurt was palpable and in many cases shaped our traditions of the faith. This longing persists for us to tap into today as a way of breathing life into ecumenical unity.

Then comes the hope part of what unifies us. When there is pain in our lives, no matter the tradition, we all turn to the same source. Saint Cyprian of Carthage, a bishop in North Africa during the Roman oppression of Christians during the 3rd century, stated that our individual pain counts as all our pain, because in truth we are united as one body in Christ. With Jesus as our head, we become one. With our relentless hope in Jesus, we find unity. The most powerful thing that can bring us together is that in the face of any sort of darkness, suffering, or pain, we are the people who declare we are in it for the long haul; we are in it for the transformative purposes of Jesus Christ in our life, the church, and ultimately all of creation. When we declare these things together, the prayer of Paul in Ephesians is answered; the cosmic-shaking "secret plan" is unveiled. When from different traditions, we are able to stand together and declare with the Psalmist, "His faithful love lasts forever," we demonstrate an unstoppable hope to the world. This is what ultimately binds us together. Jesus is real. He is alive. And together our hope is in him.

Our unity is not because we do things the same way. We each have different smells and bells. It is not because we agree on all the different tenants of Christian practice and theology. Those distinctives matter. But they must be held loosely in the face of Jesus, the Living God. Held loosely in the sense that while they are stones in our respective foundations, they are not the main foundation stone, *a la* Psalm 118:22. Where the triune God is worshipped, we, though diverse, are made into brothers from different mothers and sisters from different misters: "All who are led by God's Spirit are God's sons and daughters...we are God's children...heirs and fellow heirs with Christ" (Romans 8:14-17, CEB).

We find ourselves united by our brokenness. We find ourselves united by an awareness of our great need. And we find ourselves united in a relentless hope, by our tenacity to keep on keeping on in the person of Jesus. Then, somewhere in the midst of this unity, Jesus' prayer in John 17 is answered: "I pray they will be one, Father, just as you are in me and I am in you."

Reshaping our understanding of the real presence of the living Jesus as our pastor, leader, guide, and power opens up a whole new realm of unity within the church. And in a way not felt in years, there is something (the Spirit?) blowing in the air these days, empowering a new understanding and opportunity to work and worship together across Christian traditions. That is not to suggest that we all start to worship and look the same. But seeing each other in the light of Jesus' life and presence could open new possibilities for partnerships and presence in our communities. And frankly, this approach, through Jesus, deepens and enriches our own traditions and faith. It softens our stances on things which in the light of Jesus we see do not mean as much as we once thought. In turn, it strengthens our distinctives and uniquenesses that helps us connect with those in our communities who connect to the gospel through those particular strengths and distinctives. We really are better together. Together we can keep each other from going down silly, sometimes inappropriate rabbit holes. Conversely, we can learn from and encourage each other towards new paradigms of ministry and worship.

I heard Dr. Gordon T. Smith, president of an Evangelical university, remark at an assembly of Catholic bishops, priests, and clergy that if we had learned how to work together centuries ago, we may have stopped our respective traditions from ingraining some less-than helpful practices and beliefs into our repertoire. If Catholics had been in dialogue with the Orthodox church in a constructive way, would their theology of Mary the mother of Jesus turned out differently? If Protestants had been in constructive dialogue with the Catholics and Orthodox Church, would we have been so quick to strip the Eucharist of all its meaning and power? If the Orthodox church was in constructive dialogue with Evangelicals, would they be better prepared to share their dynamic faith and practice with non-Christians outside of their particular ethnicity? Dialogue between all of us can only strengthen us and help us discern our way forward in our unique mission with Jesus. The three main traditions of the Christian faith — Catholic, Orthodox, and Protestant — are connected by the most unifying figure there is: the person of Jesus. Around his presence we must be able to say Paul's words together:

> *[We] are one body and one spirit, just as God also called [us] in one hope. There is one Lord, one faith, one baptism, and one God and Father of all, who is over all, through all, and in all.*

> Ephesians 4:15-16

If we can say the Apostle's Creed together, we can begin to move towards reconciliation and partnership. When I repeat the creed (which ashamedly in my tradition is unusual and new) alongside my brothers and sisters in the faith, I sense the cosmic hope of which Paul spoke. I sense centuries of story, victory, trial, challenge, and successes of the Church. I am drawn into something much bigger than me. It gives perspective, and it reminds me of the unstoppable trajectory of the church empowered by Jesus' Spirit. I sense him in the room with us, smiling, and answering Paul's prayer for unity in the church. Sorry if that sounds cheesy, but I dare you to try it. Say it now aloud by yourself. As you speak it, sense the centuries of all our mothers and fathers of the faith, in all Christian traditions, giving their lives to this story. This story has captivated and empowered generations. It is the most enduring story the world has ever heard, and people from all races and places have aligned themselves with it under the headship of Christ.

> *I believe in God, the Father almighty,*
> *creator of heaven and earth.*
>
> *I believe in Jesus Christ, God's only Son, our Lord,*
> *who was conceived by the Holy Spirit,*
> *born of the Virgin Mary,*
> *suffered under Pontius Pilate,*
> *was crucified, died, and was buried;*
> *he descended to the dead.*
> *On the third day he rose again;*
> *he ascended into heaven,*
> *he is seated at the right hand of the Father,*
> *and he will come to judge the living and the dead.*
>
> *I believe in the Holy Spirit,*
> *the holy catholic Church,*
> *the communion of saints,*
> *the forgiveness of sins,*
> *the resurrection of the body,*
> *and the life everlasting. Amen.*

You just said you believe in the holy catholic church. You listed off the essentials of the Christian faith, and among them was the short version of Paul's words in Ephesians 4:5-6. One church. One body. One baptism. One faith. One Lord. And we all pledge our allegiance to him. Some of us do it in robes with smells and bells. Some of us do it on a Monday night in a bar. And some of us use overhead projectors, but we gather to worship the same guy. So simple. So powerful.

One of my favourite quotes that I return to often is from Clement of Alexandria. I put it before my church community on occasion whenever we discuss, among other things, working alongside our other brothers and sisters in the faith. Clement was introduced to me by a Dutch Reformed theology professor at an Evangelical college who leaned heavily on Catholic and Orthodox traditions. Clement did most of his writing in the late second century. He wrote tirelessly of Jesus being the person and power through which humanity could, in submission to each other and Jesus, find new hope and unity: ultimately, salvation. His desire has become mine. In any way I can, with whatever influence I have,

I will work in my little community to fulfill Paul's prayer for the Church.

> *The union of everything makes, from multiple and dispersed voices, one single divine harmony, one unique symphony conducted by the unique choirmaster*
> *who is the Logos.*

Clement of Alexandria, 3rd century Church Father

9

The Bible

Your word is a light unto my path

Psalm 119:105

Certainly what is unique to Protestants is our love of studying the Bible. Evangelicals take it up another level. You will hear much more of it read aloud in an Anglican, Catholic, or Orthodox gathering — which is great and somewhat surprising for many Evangelicals to learn — but when it comes to spending years of study in academic settings, buying commentaries, convincing our parishioners that they should read it everyday, and worrying about exegeting and preaching the best expository sermon possible, that is where Protestant pastors get the badge for their uniform. We make a big deal out of the Bible. In many of our churches you will (sadly) not see the use of artistic visuals, symbols, or icons, but the Bible remains front and centre. It is perhaps on a table at the front or at least in the preacher's hand.

Certainly its text is on the screen.

We believe the Bible is more than a book. It is more than a mere human document, though its collision of humanity and divinity is part of what makes it the unique collection of texts that it is. We use it for guidance, for understanding our faith and the world around us, and for tapping into the ancient historical and ongoing story of God and his relationship to creation and humanity. We call it the Word of God. But as my friend, Dr. Knowles, rightly asks in response to our calling it that, "In *what manner* is it the Word of God?" More on that in a moment.

I will be honest. For many years I believed that the only way to appropriately understand and teach the Word of God was to apply several methods and be a certain type of interpreter. I had to be educated. I needed to go to Bible school, seminary, and conferences. I needed smart professors to teach me how to read it, where it came from, how it was put together, and all of the details about translation from original languages and varying translation biases. I needed to be up-to-date on the most current methods of practicing textual criticism. I knew that if an application or lesson from a text did not take into account the original context and the best guess at authorial intent, it was likely off the mark. I knew where to find the best commentaries, books, and journal articles. I knew who was a good biblical studies author and expert and who was not. Then, if I had all of this in place, I could masterfully exegete the text, preach great sermons, and wow my friends and parishioners with expert analysis.

I still believe all of that is good practice and a great honour and privilege for those of us who get to have these experiences and study Scripture in such a way. But Jesus has also messed with me enough times now that while I still hold those practices and methods in high regard, I have had to make room for a few other methods in reading and interpreting Scripture. Most of us would say that God can use anything to communicate with us. He is, after all, the God who used an ass to get someone's attention. God will use nature, other people, even angels. Yet for some reason some of us have a difficult time with Scripture being used "outside" of the bounds of good academic exegetical practice.

It was during my discovery of listening prayer and journaling that Jesus started to teach me another method. It is a mysterious method of applying Scripture. It requires the listening ear of my church community to help me hear what I am supposed to hear. But it is a beautiful demonstration of just how intimate Jesus will be in leading and loving us.

On one particular day in the midst of my depression and anxiety — after the wall — we were seeing some people off at our door who had just dropped a meal off for us (our little church took remarkable care of us during that dark time). Out of nowhere, as we were saying good-bye to them, this voice in my head started saying "Numbers 23." It kept entering my thoughts. Numbers 23. Numbers 23. Numbers 23.

Perhaps you have the book of Numbers memorized. I do not. Perhaps you know the content of Numbers well enough to know where things are located. I did not. I walked back to our couch where I spent most of the days sitting, reading my Bible, praying, and journaling. I opened my Bible to Numbers 23 and began to read. I was stunned.

While Shalene walked through the dark aftermath of the cancer diagnosis, the anxiety, and the fear, Alison (the prophet from chapter three) sensed that God was using that time to shape her into someone new — to form a new confidence rooted in her awareness of God's love for her. One of the great troubles Shalene had had for years was believing that God could be a good father. She had no trouble connecting with Jesus and the Spirit, but her relationship with God the Father was distant and broken. She did not trust him. For Shalene, the cancer diagnosis was only confirmation that God could not be trusted and that he did not love her. Alison sensed all of this and spent many hours praying and talking Shalene through these feelings and false beliefs. During several of our visits with Alison she would pray the imagery of a lioness over Shalene. Alison felt that God was birthing in Shalene a new spirit that would rise up and roar like a lioness, empowered by the great never-ending love of God the Good Father. Not surprisingly, it was hard for Shalene to believe any of this considering her current state of mind. Seeing that most days were spent in an overwhelming state of fear and anxiety, it was hard to picture herself as a Spirit-filled lioness full of courage and strength.

A big part of my journey through that dark period was learning to trust the intimacy of God's Spirit and voice within me — learning to trust that Jesus was real and was my pastor. Through the journaling and listening prayer, through the crazy challenges that Shalene and I were facing, I continued to wrestle with my doubt about the "realness" of everything. Could I trust Jesus' voice? Could I trust that it was real? Could I act on the conversations I was having with Jesus? This was the great struggle of my faith.

So when I opened my Bible to Numbers 23, my assumption was that I would find a boring list, not a deeply intimate message from God to me. Keep in mind the lioness imagery. Keep in mind my struggle about believing, trusting, and acting on the voice of Jesus. Now take a moment and read Numbers 23. Then read chapter 24. And while you are reading, as odd as this might sound, don't think about the story being told, think about my story and Shalene's story. What do you see? Go ahead and read it now before continuing on.

(Insert Jeopardy gameshow music here)

Can you see why I found this fascinating?
Can you see why this messed with me?

Numbers 23:12 He answered and said, "Don't I have to take care to speak whatever the Lord gives me to say?"

Then Balaam raised his voice and made his address:
"Arise, Balak, and listen;
   hear me out, Zippor's son.
God isn't a man that he would lie,
   or a human being that he would change his mind.
Has he ever spoken and not done it,
   or promised and not fulfilled it?
I received a blessing, and he blessed.

> *I can't take it back.*
> *He hasn't envisioned misfortune for Jacob,*
> > *nor has he seen trouble for Israel.*
> *The Lord his God is with him,*
> > *proclaimed as his king.*
> *God, who brought them out of Egypt,*
> > *is like a magnificent wild bull for him.*
> *There is no omen against Jacob,*
> > *no divination against Israel.*
> *Instantly it is told to Jacob,*
> > *and to Israel, what God performs.*
> *A people now rises like a lioness,*
> > *like a lion it stands up.*
> *It doesn't lie down until it eats the prey*
> > *and drinks the blood of the slain."*

Numbers 23:18-24

> *He crouched and lay down like a lion;*
> > *like a lioness, who can make her rise?*

Numbers 24:9a

Coincidence?
Or intimacy?

This is what I immediately went and wrote in my journal that evening:

Numbers 23. Why? I have no idea. I hadn't been thinking about Numbers and certainly don't know any of the stories in Numbers. So I went and read it and couldn't believe what I was reading, particularly 23:12, 18-26, 24:9. It's like God is yelling at us over and over again that we can trust his promises, that I can hear his voice when I'm open to hearing it, and that I must "take care to speak whatever the Lord gives me to say" (23:12). Incredible. Thank-you, Jesus! You are on the move; your glory is incredible; your presence is undeniable; you're revealing yourself in ways that demand my faith, trust, and belief. Help me continue to grow, Jesus! Help me continue to trust you. Teach me, Jesus! Like a gentle master, teach me!

This sort of biblical application breaks all the rules. I ripped the text from its context. I made it all about me and my story. I did not put any effort into study. I did not care at all about what the original author may have been trying to do. I picked the verses that I needed to hear and pretty much ignored the rest. I did something potentially dangerous by just about everyone's standards. But I cannot deny the restorative, powerful, redemptive, and gracious act of God I sensed within that experience.

Like I said, I stand by all of the best practices for interpreting and teaching Scripture. But I have also come to realize that God will use this incredibly unique collection of writings to demonstrate his intimacy with us in ways that break those rules. Certainly within this rule-breaking method of using Scripture there are still some best practices. Tell your story to others and let them critique it. I immediately told this story to a few friends. This practice helps to make sure you do not start a cult. That is important. More seriously, it provides another place for affirmation or sober second thought. The best of our ongoing transformation is done in community. It may also confirm and affirm what the Spirit is doing in those around you. When we shared this story with Alison, it encouraged her and reaffirmed her sense of what God was saying to her.

I did, eventually, do the work of exegesis on the Numbers 23 story which meant I also read chapter 22. And there it was — the story of the ass. I had to laugh at God's sense of humour in working out his providence in my life. If he can use an ass, he can certainly use his Word to grab my attention.

The point of that Numbers 23 story is not entirely about opening ourselves up to the idea of Jesus using Scripture to pastor us in ways outside of our typical training or understanding of proper, careful exegesis. That was important for me. It may be for you, too. But perhaps more importantly it serves as a good illustration of the hierarchy of Jesus and Scripture. Scripture serves Jesus, not the other way around. Jesus did not come to give us the Bible. He came to reveal himself, and he gave us the Spirit. *Sola Scriptura* — by Scripture alone — cannot mean that Christians only need the Bible. If that were the case it renders Jesus' giving of the Spirit unnecessary in terms of guidance to the church and believers. To suggest that by scripture alone we understand our Christian faith is simply neither true nor helpful. The real life presence of Jesus in the world, in our life together as community, and in us personally is how we understand our faith. Scripture serves this purpose, it does not supplant it.

When Dr. Knowles asks his students the question, "In *what manner* is the Bible the Word of God?" he is conveying the essence of what I am attempting to explain. We read the text, but those of us who approach it aware of its uniqueness and capability as *something more*, know that the text also reads us. It is mysteriously made alive by the Spirit. It speaks. At its best, reading scripture is a conversation. This is why so many of us find the black and white process of proof-texting and the militant defence of certain aspects of the book's historicity or perceived scientific authority to be so irrelevant to the conversation. Those are answers to questions I am not interested in asking.

Scripture is alive. The book speaks. The book can take us into the throne room. It reveals to us how the Living God has interacted with history. I like how Dr. David Fitch refers to Scripture as "The Family Photo Album." It talks to us about the lived history of our mothers, fathers, uncles, aunts, and cousins of the faith. They walked with the Living God. They heard him. They saw him. As readers today, we join the conversation.

This could be why practices such as Lectio Devina have been rediscovered in many settings. Prayer before, and with, the text creates space for the Spirit to use the Bible as a means of revelation, ultimately directing our gaze to Jesus. Again, this does not mean dismissing the good practice and hard work of exegesis, especially in community, but it does provide another opportunity for Scripture to speak.

The Franciscan friar, Richard Rohr, reminds us that Jesus, the human and divine man, empowered and led by the Spirit, is our hermeneutic for reading Scripture. We read the Bible along and with Jesus. I am convinced more and more that Jesus, because of his intimate connection with us and our particular local church, is interested in helping us read Scriptures in ways specific to our context. He knows where we are at. He knows where our church must be pushed, challenged, and encouraged. He knows how to help us read the text in the way we need. Perhaps this sounds too myopic. It may also sound dangerous. However, I am trying to admit and own what we too often deny and dismiss. Rohr remarks, "*How you see is what you see*; the *who* that you bring to your reading of the Scriptures matters."[1] We must admit that we bring our baggage to the text. But if we allow Jesus to help us carry our baggage to the text, he, being our pastor and Good Shepherd, will also know how to sensitively help us unpack it before the sacred text. Do we trust that he is alive and walking with us alongside the text? Do we trust that he is for us? Do we trust that his Spirit will guide us ever deeper into the truth? If so, then if we come as submissive readers in community with our brothers and sisters and Jesus, especially as we walk within an ecumenical framework as mentioned previously, we can trust that he will guide our exegesis and application for his redemptive purposes. The dynamic of the Spirit-filled life must include our reading of Scripture. If it becomes purely academic in the sense that all mystery is lost and that all reality of the present tutor, Jesus, is dismissed, then we are left as arrogant interpreters

---

1 https://cac.org/jesus-interpreted-scripture-2017-01-10/

who believe that we alone can master the revelation. It is then that we lower the Word of God to a simple textbook, guidebook, handbook, or list of "dos and don'ts."

Let me complicate matters even further. Why are we afraid of interpreting Scripture the way Jesus and the early church apostles, fathers, and mothers did? We have been helped immensely by textual criticism. Yet this focus has also been stunting in some ways. The Reformation and enlightenment made us believe there was a way to interpret that would always "figure it out." Our lawyer forefathers in the Reformation did what they knew how to do: they systematized things in such a way to remove the mysterious and any sort of ambiguity. We gained so much from this. Modern Evangelical scholarship owes that era a debt of gratitude. However, the outcome extinguished the art of approaching Scripture and replaced it with a science. Is there not room for both approaches working together? Can we embrace the best practices of textual criticism, contextual analysis, and academic rigour while also embracing the divine and mysterious art of interacting with the Living Word?

Jesus broke the rules of textual criticism all the time. It seems he had no issue ripping Old Testament passages from their context. He could do so because he lived in a real-time dynamic relationship with the Spirit. The safeguard in his approach to Scripture was his connection to the Father through the Spirit (John 10:30 & 12:49).

A great example of Jesus' seemingly questionable exegesis exists in John 19:28-30. Jesus says that what happened to him was done so that Scripture would be fulfilled. He appears to be referencing Psalm 69:21. Wow. That is quite the connection to make. If someone made a similar connection and claim today they would probably be accused of twisting Scripture to fit their agenda.

Think about Matthew's suggestion that the whole Judas scenario was done to fulfill the prophecy of Jeremiah.

> *The chief priests picked up the silver pieces and said, "According to the Law it's not right to put this money in the treasury. Since it was used to pay for someone's life, it's unclean." So they decided to use it to buy the potter's field where strangers could be buried. That's why that field is called "Field of Blood" to this very day. This fulfilled the words of Jeremiah the prophet: And I took the thirty pieces of silver, the price for the one whose price had been set by some of the Israelites, and I gave them for the potter's field, as the Lord commanded me.*

> Matthew 27:6-10

First of all, it looks like Zechariah 11:12-13 is a better fit than Jeremiah 32:6-9. Second, by our standards today, we would consider this interpretation terrible exegetical work by Matthew. Go back and read those passages. It is hard to see a solid connection between what was happening during the prophet's writing and what took place after Jesus' death.

You could rightly accuse Jesus and his early followers of confirmation bias if you so wanted. They would all fail today's biblical interpretation classes in seminary. Or you could say that they approached Scripture through the eyes of the Spirit who helped them interpret it for their time and benefit.

This sounds terribly risky and dangerous. I get it. But it is the risk of faith, that Jesus is alive and interested in joining us in these real-time tasks of the Christian faith, like reading the Bible. Yes, it must be done in community. Yes, it must be done alongside the best practices of biblical scholarship. Yes, it must be done with great humility and surrender. But we cannot remove our pastor from pastoring us through the canon.

R.W. Moberly, an incredible biblical scholar, states that Scripture must be "something before which one lingers long and ponders expectantly, with that particular kind of openness which is called prayer."[2] Ears to hear and eyes to see must be our prayer in reading and interpreting Scripture. This sort of discovery and interpretation, always done in partnership with our academic study, our commitment to discussion within the broader church, is where we create space for the Spirit to lead us in the Bible. We must sit long before the text. We must ponder. We must discuss. We pray. We do it alone. We do it in community. We expect to be transformed, not simply enlightened. In the process we expect to meet with God through his Spirit so that we become more and more a reflection of Jesus.

---

2 How May We Speak of God? A Reconsideration of the Nature of Biblical Theology. *Tyndale Bulletin*. 53.2 (2002)

Contrary to many of our Evangelical statements concerning Scripture, the greatest source of authority in the Word of God is not its historicity or our concern with its inerrancy, but rather our ability to submit to the active Spirit of God who comes to the text with us and who is alive in the text. We must come to the text knowing that by his grace, love, and mercy, *we are known* through our reading of the text. Jesus pursues us in the text as we pursue him. If we approach the text with a willingness to be broken before it and broken because of it, Jesus can touch us through it.

My story from Numbers 23 is not good exegesis, but it was certainly God using the text to speak to me. Is it sermon material? Not in the expository sense. Was it confirmed by mature Christians around me? Yes. Did it draw me closer to Jesus? Yes. Could he have used something else to do the same thing? Sure. But instead he used Scripture and drew me deeper into its divine sacred mystery. Losing yourself every once and while in the family photo album is a good thing.

Jesus is there.

Moving Forward

10

Nurturing a Life with *the* Pastor

SELECTED STORIES

Christian leaders cannot simply be persons who have well-informed opinions about the burning issues of our time. Their leadership must be rooted in the permanent, intimate relationship with the incarnate Word, Jesus, and they need to find there the source for their words, advice, and guidance. Through the discipline of contemplative prayer, Christian leaders have to learn to listen again and again to the voice of love and to find there the wisdom and courage to address whatever issue presents itself to them.

Henry Nouwen, *In the Name of Jesus*

Ending this book with this chapter is very intentional. The book could have started here, too, but if you are anything like me, you breeze through the personal formation stuff and get right into the how-do-I-do-it sections. But I cannot stress this enough: you will run dry so quickly trying to do any of the things I have discussed so far if you do not learn how to foster this Jesus-as-our-pastor stuff on your own. Doubt will overwhelm you if your experience is not as profound as you would have hoped. The fear of being a phoney who is trying to pull the wool over everyone's eyes will rage inside your head and heart if you do not have any lived experience of your own. This is not a game you can play unless you can recognize and embrace the moments in your own life when Jesus has undeniably been with you, teaching you, and demonstrating his compassion for you and his creation.

This journey of faith is full of ups and downs. Sometimes the things we hope for happen. Sometimes they do not. Leading a church which chases intimacy with Jesus and has a belief that he is alive and speaks today can be hard. Sometimes it does not *feel* like he is alive and speaking. I can tell you that I believe God is always up to something even when I do not *feel* it, but to go on for days, months, and years without stories of Jesus' living presence in our midst can make it an almost unbearable grind.

I know that Jesus does not "show up," even though we use that language. I know that we do not need to invite the presence of the Spirit into our midst, even though we do. I think using language like that can be unhelpful, but it is also indicates our heart's desires. We want Jesus to meet with us. And sometimes our language, though not representative of the best theology, is simply human and reflects an authentic deep yearning inside of us.

And so it is that we, as pastors, must nurture space in our life where we can slow down enough to intentionally listen and see. We will have our doubts and we will have our frustrations, but if we lose hope that Jesus is alive — if we lose our craziness — our leadership will become so arduous for ourselves and those around us that the weight will eventually crush us. I do not say it that way to sound over-dramatic; I say it that way because I know the feeling intimately. Sometimes we will make the space to see and hear. Sometimes God will make the space. And sometimes life just has a way of being so good or bad that it puts us in that space. But make no mistake, we need those spaces. I wonder how far Moses would have gone into the desert — how long he would have dealt with those people or his own self-doubt and fear — had he not had his mountaintop experience?

Ideally we would each foster these spaces on our own and we would nurture our ability to have eyes to see and ears to hear, but that is not the way it started for me. Sometimes in God's grace, or perhaps his mercy, we land in the midst of an opportunity. Shortly after the coffeeshop discussion and hitting the wall, and not too long after the cancer diagnosis, the seizures, and the terrible months that followed, life created the space for God to grab a hold of me. I know that before all of that stuff happened, God was always trying to get my attention, but for whatever reason, this season was different.

As I confessed earlier, Jesus had been, for me, someone to emulate, not someone to whom I could listen. He was an idea, not a person. He was a belief, not a friend. He was someone I taught about, but not someone I knew. What follows are a few of the stories of how that all changed.

To be exact, eight prefacing stories are required to properly illustrate this journey and personal shift, before relaying the final story.

Preface story one.

In late 2012, around the same time as my coffeeshop experience with Lee, the Ancaster Ministerial Association, in which I was a participant, had a meeting where we were deciding what to do for the 2013 Lenten Lunch series we hosted and ran in our community. For seven weeks during Lent we would host a lunch and provide a short Lent-themed devotional. About 80 wonderful senior-citizens from the community showed up each week.

We distributed the dates for each devotional we would each speak on and decided that the series would focus on the seven miracles of Jesus from the Gospel of John. I received my date and plugged it into my calendar. I received my Scripture text and put it in a folder, not to be thought of again until a few days before I had to speak.

Preface story two.

Shalene's favourite flower is the tulip. And here is something sad: I did not know that until later in this story. Chalk one up for the husband of the year.

Preface story three.

February 7, 2013: the day of the diagnosis. As I mentioned, we fell apart on this day. Days turned into weeks that turned into months, during which time you would have usually found us crumpled in a ball in front of our fireplace, in bed, or barely getting through each day. We went to counselling. We had a steady flow of amazing people coming to care for us. I lost 30 pounds from not eating. Our kids were suffering. We had so many questions. We spent hours in tears and desperate prayer. Some of my worst moments included contemplating driving our vehicle, with my family in it, into oncoming traffic. Yes, it was that bad.

Preface story four.

On the night of February 7th, Alison the Prophet and her husband Rod came over to be with and pray for us. As mentioned earlier, part of Alison's ministry to Shalene in these days was being compelled to tell Shalene that somehow in the midst of the journey ahead, God was going to help her realize just how much he loved her. As I mentioned earlier, this was an extremely significant and challenging idea for Shalene. Shalene feared God. Getting cancer seemed only a validation of this deep internal fear that had festered in her mind since childhood. Her experiences had contributed to her distrust in God's love for her. Accepting Jesus and the Spirit was easy for Shalene. But Father God was not someone to be trusted.

Preface story five.

During several of our personal journaling and listening prayer times, both Shalene and I felt like Jesus was telling us that the coming of spring had something to do with our healing: Shalene's physical healing, my son's seizures, and all of our emotional healing. This puzzled us, but we clung to it. You cling to anything when you are that low.

One morning during a time of journaling, Shalene began to think about our circumstances as a time of trial, testing, and intentional shaping. She felt compelled to count the days between her diagnosis and the first day of spring. It just so happened to be 40 days. She mentioned this to me and I responded with an intrigued but casual shrug of the shoulders. Most days, despite my desire to find and cling to hope, the anxiety and depression overwhelmed everything and made life a fog of tiredness, sluggishness, and contempt for most things.

Preface story six.

Several weeks after her diagnosis, Shalene was reading through the Gospel of John. She read John 9:1-7.

> *As Jesus walked along, he saw a man who was blind from birth. Jesus' disciples asked, "Rabbi, who sinned so that he was born blind, this man or his parents?" Jesus answered, "Neither he nor his parents. This happened so that God's mighty works might be displayed in him. While it's daytime, we must do the works of him who sent me. Night is coming*

when no one can work. While I am in the world, I am the light of the world." After he said this, he spit on the ground, made mud with the saliva, and smeared the mud on the man's eyes. Jesus said to him, "Go, wash in the pool of Siloam" (this word means sent). So the man went away and washed. When he returned, he could see.

Reading her own sickness into the story, she read the story aloud to me and then asked what I thought. I said this: "I will tell you what I think. I think it is stupid. If God wants to make us sick just so that he can show up and make himself look good, then he can keep his goodness to himself. I do not ever want to hear that story again." And that was that.

Preface story seven.

A couple of weeks later I remembered that I had to speak at the upcoming Lenten lunch service. I was not doing much of anything work-related, but I was trying to keep up with some responsibilities so I could continue to get a paycheque. I had not looked at my assigned passage when I received it so I had no idea what it was. I went into my office, picked up my Ancaster Ministerial Association folder, opened it, and found the passage on which I was to speak. It was John 9:1-7. I thought, *"Are you kidding me?"*! I was angry. Really angry. Begrudgingly, I sat down, pulled out some commentaries, and began to read. Slowly my eyes started to open to a teaching that I had not grasped upon first reading.

We all want to know "why?". Why does crap happen? The disciples' question is often our question. Did I do something? Is this a consequence for something? But Jesus essentially sidesteps that line of questioning. His response is concerning what he is going to do right now. When Jesus says "This happened...," I suspect he is referring to what he is about to do. He is about to show his power, love, and presence by intervening into the brokenness of humanity and doing something crazy. He is about to give people a story — a story that will demonstrate to the world that The Light of the World is in our midst.

I began to get excited. Though still incredibly anxious and depressed about my own circumstances, I found hope in this story. And hope was something I found hard to come by or accept during that time.

Preface story eight.

The night before I was to speak at the Lenten lunch was a bad night in the Gerrard home. Shalene and I put the kids to bed and then collapsed again on the living room floor. Our anxiety was through the roof. We sat in fear and tears. And then I did something I had never done before. As I knelt on the ground I began to pray: "God, I need something I have never asked for before. I need an angel. I need you to send someone to tell me that everything is going to be okay. It was really great of you to send an angel to tell those around Jesus' empty tomb that it was going to be okay. Well I need something like that. I am so desperate."

Of course in my mind this angel needed to be big, wearing a

bright white gown, and ideally with a flashing billboard over its head reading, "I am an angel." Trumpets would have been nice, too. But to be honest, I had little expectation of this sort of prayer being answered. And with that, we made our way to bed.

Finally, the story.

The next day I got ready for the Lenten lunch. It was a cold, snowy, and blustery Southern Ontario day — the kind of day that makes a bad mood even worse. As I was getting ready, Shalene reminded me of something: that day, March 20th, was the first day of spring. It was 40 days after the day of the diagnosis. I guess I knew it, but I did not want to think about it because I was pretty convinced I was going to be let down — that it was going to be like any other day filled with worry, anxiety, depression, and doubt. But so it was, the first day of spring: a snowy, cold, blustery, and crappy day.

I arrived at the church where the event was being hosted. I went and sat down at a table awaiting my time to go up and speak the message I had prepared. A petite elderly woman came and sat down beside me. We exchanged names, though for the life of me I cannot remember hers. I did not think anything of this new acquaintance and when my time came to speak, I got up and instantly forgot I had even met the woman. I shared a bit of our story since Shalene's diagnosis, my first run-in with the text from John, and then my understanding of the text upon doing some research. And although I shared how the text gave me hope, I did not shy away from saying that I was still filled with worry and anxiety. I finished speaking and took my seat. When I returned to my table I did not notice that the old woman was no longer there.

When the service concluded I was greeted by several well-meaning people who came over to give me a hug and offer their support. I admit that all I wanted to do was get home and go back to bed. And then it happened.

The petite elderly woman returned. She stood behind me and tapped me on the shoulder. I turned around and she held out a large bouquet of flowers. Tulips, to be exact. She looked into my eyes and said, "I want you to give these to your wife. Tell her spring is coming and everything is going to be okay. I have to go now. Someone is waiting for me." Then she smiled and left.

"Where on earth did she get these flowers from?" was all I thought. She certainly did not go outside and pick them in the snow. I left the church and returned home.

When I got home I gave the flowers to Shalene and told her what the woman had said. Neither of us thought much of it except that it was a little bizarre that this lady had a bunch of tulips on hand.

Later that day, we had planned to have some friends over, and it just happened to be Alison and Rod. As we sat down in the living room together they asked us how our day was (knowing that most of our days were pretty awful). I began to tell them about my day — the speaking, the little old woman, the flowers — and then Shalene stopped me.

"Aaron, do you remember what you prayed about last night?"

We both looked at each other, like what the heck just happened here? And slowly we began to remember all of the prefacing stories that I just shared with you. One by one we reminded each other of the moments along the journey: the conversations, the journaling, the connecting dots — all of it.

Our friend's eyes lit up. "Don't you see it?" Alison asked. "He is chasing you; he is wooing you; he is revealing himself all around you; he is answering you with angels. He gave you flowers!"

Our eyes filled with tears. We still had a long way to go with the anxiety, the questions, and the doubts. But on that day — the first day of spring — God sent us a messenger and brought us tulips. He told us everything was going to be okay.

Another Story

As spring eventually came and the temperature began to warm, I wish I could say that everything turned around for Shalene and me. It did not. Despite what God was doing around us, the anxiety and depression were still running their course and we had a ways to go. Shalene was taking the cancer and the appointments week by week, the same went for my son's seizure appointments, and my correspondence with the Canadian Revenue Agency continued as we tried to figure out what had happened. Life was hardly back to normal.

At one point later in spring I ended up in a doctor's office answering questions about suicide. Our counsellor had become very concerned for me, so in collaboration with our doctor, I was prescribed medication to try and get my brain to function out of the darkness. The day I was prescribed those pills was a bad day. I felt like a total failure, like I had let everyone around me down, and that I had become one of *those* people: needy, broken, and weak. I hated that bottle of pills. Shalene took me home from the doctor's office, I put the pills in our medicine cabinet, and despite the advice of everyone around me, I swore I would never take them. I went to bed angry and anxious, hoping I would not wake up in the morning. I felt like there was a battle in my gut for who I was and who I would be moving forward. I just wanted it all to end; I had no strength left to decide who I wanted to win the battle for Aaron.

When I did wake up, it was a morning I will never forget. There was a voice in my head: a distinct voice. And it said one thing over and over again: "I am going to give you flowers." I knew it was God. Even still, I became very angry. I was angry to the point that by the time I crawled out of bed and into the shower, I was saying aloud, "If you do not give me flowers today, then that is it; I am out. I will give it all up and I will never return to you." Yet the voice persisted louder and louder: "I am going to give you flowers."

The only reason I had got out of bed that morning was because I had to drag myself to a dentist appointment in the early afternoon. Yes, I would have normally stayed in bed until the *late* afternoon.

I arrived at the dentist's office, checked in, and waited for my turn. Eventually the dental hygienist came and got me and took me to my chair. I settled in, answered, "I am fine," to the hygienist's question of, "How are you doing?" and waited for them to bib me up and lower me down.

As I waited, I looked to my left and there they were. Flowers. Well, sort of. On the wall were framed photos of flowers. You would think that was the moment when I realized God was real, that the voice was real, and that God loved me. But it just made me more angry. "Is this really the best you can do?" I said in my head. "You are supposed to be the God of the Universe, and the best you can do is some lame photos on a dentist's wall?" I was fuming on the inside. I was starting to give up.

I finished at the dentist, went home, and sat outside on our back deck waiting for the day to be over. I am not sure if I noticed that Shalene and the kids were not at home, but either way I had not seen anyone when I got there.

Only a few minutes later I heard the sliding screen door open from the back of our house onto the deck. Two sets of little feet quickly ran across the deck to me. I did not look up; I only continued to stare at the ground between my feet. Suddenly, directly under my face and into my gaze stretched two hands, one from my son and one from my daughter. In each hand was small bunch of flowers. "Daddy, daddy, we want you to have these." I was stunned. In case you are wondering, no, my family does not usually bring me flowers. Ever. I looked up into the doorway where my wife was standing. I asked, "Why?" She told me that while driving home from wherever they were, the kids saw wild flowers growing in a ditch. They immediately began yelling to pull over because "we need to pick some flowers for daddy today!" Shalene is not in the habit of pulling over on the side of the road to pick flowers, but on this day she did. The kids picked flowers and brought them home to me. They were so happy about it. All I could muster in my heart was to say "thank-you" to God.

That night before bed I took my medication for the first time. I was taking some necessary steps to get healthy again. And I had a sense I could do it because no matter how deep the depression was and how little hope I had, I could not escape the pursuit of God's love. Like Shalene before me, I got flowers from God. Amazing.

I told Shalene that night about my experience. While you might expect that she would be encouraged, she was disappointed. She wanted some more flowers. Where was her gift?

The next morning Shalene woke up with a similar experience of a voice in her head. Though instead of hearing a voice saying she would receive flowers, her promise was that she would get a rainbow. The problem was, as she looked outside of our bedroom window, there was not a cloud in the sky; it was a beautiful sunny day. There was nothing about that day or the forecast that made a rainbow seem likely.

Shalene went about her day taking care of the kids. The morning was typical. Lunch came and went. And then the kids went outside to play. After all, it was a beautiful day.

All of the sudden Shalene heard our oldest begin to scream.

"Mommy! Mommy!" came the cry from the front yard, so loud that Shalene could clearly hear it in the house. She ran outside expecting to find someone with a badly scrapped knee or the kids in a wrestling match gone bad. Instead, she found a rainbow.

Our son had pulled the garden hose onto the driveway and was shooting water up into the sky. As the sun beamed through the spray of water, a large rainbow appeared which was delighting the kids to the point of them needing to be sure the whole world knew what was happening. Shalene stood there taking it all in, amazed that God would demonstrate his love in such a way.

These were not the only times God used our children to speak to us. They were an instrument quite often. I remember asking them why they did those things, and their response was simple: we just did. Could it be that children are more easily obedient when God nudges them to do something? They lack our adult skepticism and doubt, I think. When the thickness of my head and my fear and doubt were too strong, God used the people who were willing to say "yes." That will forever be a great challenge and inspiration to me.

Flowers came out of nowhere. Rainbows came on a sunny day. God had a way of demonstrating his love when it looked like there was no way he could. These were beautiful metaphors for what he was doing in our life. Where there was little hope, he stepped in to say he was there with us. He is all around us. He is good. He is loving. He is with us. And the same Jesus who said, "This happened so that God's mighty works might be displayed in him," is still at it. He is still doing his thing and giving us stories to tell.

Someone asked me recently what it is that holds me to my faith. I replied that when everything is stripped away, all I have are my stories. Looking back to that conversation with Lee in the coffee shop, I believe now that the only way God could use me to lead a church where the unexplainable and mysterious could be a part of our story, was to walk with me through these experiences. Now I have stories. I have a testimony of God's loving presence that I never had before. These stories are what I go back to when things are dry, frustrating, or downright maddening. When my skepticism is high, when doubt runs wild, and when fear of my potential craziness sets in, I remind myself of when I met Jesus.

When I am in the darkness, I do my best to remember what I know to be true in the light. I remember the stories.

Sure, you can read these stories and call them simple coincidence. Faith demands that I say you could be right. It could all be confirmation bias. But faith also gives me the space to say, no, there is something to this. I believe there is a God who is still in the business of entering into our good, bad, and ugly, and giving us signs and wonders that always point back to himself and his goodness. I believe we have to nurture this sort of stuff in our life. We must continue to cry out, "Lord, give me eyes to see you and ears to hear you!"

How to Nurture Your Stories

(WITHOUT NEEDING YOUR LIFE TO FALL APART)

I read a book during my time at seminary, by Andrew Purves titled, *Pastoral Theology in the Classical Tradition*. In mining several of the church fathers' reflections on pastoral ministry, Purves noted common threads. I found these threads powerful then, but it was during all of these experiences that I began to understand and feel them far more intimately.

> Ministry is not 'natural' work in the sense that it is within our human compass and possibility. It is, in a sense, an alien work that demands great transformation by God, for the want of which the work of the pastor cannot succeed. In fact, the lack of interior renewal will lead to an outward ministry that will likely destroy both the pastor and his or her congregation.[1]

How do we do it? First, slow down. I was surprised to find out that one of the benefits of my depression and pretty much shutting down was that it stopped me from *doing*. I did not do much at all. This is not a recipe for life, but it did help me to realize that the opposite is true, too: being busy and constantly doing is also not good practice. I have heard it said that the real miracle of Moses and the burning bush was not that the bush was on fire and did not burn; rather, that Moses saw it in the first place.[2] He could

---

1 Westminster John Knox Press, 2001. Page 118
2 Exodus 3:2b

have walked right past it and kept doing his shepherding job. Think about it. At first glance you would think that everyone would see a burning bush that is not burning up, but when you reflect on your life, how many times have you missed a miracle? I suggest it happens to us all of the time. God is at work all around us, but we are busy. Burning bushes are easy to walk past. Nurturing an intentional slow paced routine-time — sometimes doing nothing at all — is so essential to being able to see what God is doing and hear what he is saying. Have you ever slowed down? Intentionally? Have you ever tried to do nothing? It is incredibly hard. It is also not celebrated in our culture. The temptation to get defensive or hide what can be seen by others as laziness can be enough to stop you from ever doing this. But we must. Nurturing space to see and hear God builds up our ability to see him in the hectic pace of life, too, because we have learned to expect it.

My mom likes watching birds. I used to mock her for this because it seemed like a nerdy thing to do. Be careful when you do that. As I began to get healthier and come out of my depression and darkness, I fell in love with sitting and watching birds. It was a new space and solitary act I created to slow down, to pray, to listen, and to see God at work. Becoming a nerdy bird watcher has changed the way I live my life. There have always been birds around. Birds did not come into existence when I got healthy. But I saw them for the first time. I now have eyes to see. I see them even when I am not purposefully looking for them.

The second thing I would suggest you do is practice listening prayer. Take the idea of prayer being a conversation — something we all believe it to be — to its natural conclusion: that God speaks and you can hear him. The Spirit *will* speak to you. She always has something to say, even if it is as simple (and profound) as, "I love you."

Ask yourself this: have you ever heard God say your name? The best Moses got was the trail God left behind.[3] We have the Holy Spirit, a person living and alive in us. Clark Pinnock remarks in his book, *Flame of Love: A Theology of the Holy Spirit*,[4] that the Holy Spirit is God's face turned toward us. While Moses saw only "God's back," the Spirit delights in introducing us to the face of God. This takes conversation to a whole new level. In our hearts and minds we can hear God speak to us. He addresses us personally. In a figurative way, we sit down with him as the first century disciples sat at the feet of Jesus.

For me, the easiest way I have engaged in this is through prayer journaling. I have a file on my computer. I write in regular font, and when I turn on the italics I change to listening mode. And God and I have a conversation. If what I am hearing comes from a place of fear, darkness, or condemnation, I dismiss it. If what I am hearing comes from a place of tenderness, love, compassion, and encouragement, I immediately write it down. Rarely do I sense more of the former than the latter. I do not question what I am writing down until after I have written it down. In the process of listening I just go with it, trusting, as I would in a "normal" conversation with a person, that I am hearing them

---

3 Exod 33:19f
4 Intervarsity Press, 1996.

as they talk to me. As I go back and re-read, there is a process of discernment that I practice and get better at where I ask myself, does that sound more like me or like the Spirit? It is a process at which I continuously learn and get better. We will always write in a style that reflects our own personality even while we hear Jesus speaking. This is, after all, what we see in Scripture. Though spirit inspired, Paul sounds a bit like Paul, Isaiah sounds like Isaiah, Matthew sounds like Matthew, and so on. The point is that we must take seriously the idea that the Spirit will speak, is with us, is for us, and will always guide us towards truth.

Often one of the ways I know that God is speaking to me is because I will write out several paragraphs of my concerns, requests, fears, or whatever, and the Spirit's response often goes into my heart in a way I never saw it coming. For example, I can write about my need for help in an upcoming task, and what I hear Jesus say in return to me is something like, "I think you need to go home and have a coffee with Shalene for half an hour." If I then chose to be obedient, I find that what I needed — what Shalene needed — was that coffee and chat. The Spirit knows me. She knows my circumstances. She knows what I need. She knows how to speak into my character, maturation process, and ongoing transformation as a human being shaped into the likeness of Christ. From these experiences and practices I continue to build my foundation as a pastor, husband, dad, friend, or fill-in-the-blank, from a place of intimacy with Jesus. My intentional times of conversation with Jesus are when I am pastored, healed, shaped, and changed. They are another testimony of Jesus' presence and power in my life.

If this idea of listening prayer is new to you then I suggest you get a copy of Brad Jersak's book, *Can You Hear me? Tuning Into the God Who Speaks*.[5] Jersak builds a theological and biblical foundation for this sort of experience, and offers excellent practical helps and exercises. He answers expected questions and presents an extremely compelling case for why a life of listening prayer ought to be our norm as Christians.

Finally, keep doing what you have been doing, always moving forward. I have said that leadership is important and you ought to be trained well as a leader. Keep going to seminars. Keep reading. Keep studying. Keep going to school. But learn to re-frame these activities within all we have been talking about. Allowing Jesus to pastor you and nurturing spaces and ways to see God's signs of love around you will keep you grounded in these other activities. He will call you back to himself when needed. He will encourage humility when you start believing too much of your own positive press. Conversely, he will encourage you when you start believing too much of your own negative press. He will remind you whose child you are, the story he is telling in and through your life, and how he sees you.

So may you receive your flowers and rainbows. They are there for you to see. May you hear Jesus. He is someone to listen to, not merely someone to emulate.

And may you let Jesus pastor you.
He will if you let him.

---

[5] Fresh Wind Press, 2012.

CONCLUSION

I sit writing this ending almost five years to the day that Shalene received her cancer diagnosis. It is another cold winter day just like that one. It is hard to believe so much time has passed by and since a good many of the stories I have shared with you occurred. I tremble saying this, but there is a part of me that misses those days. I hated them. I would never wish those feelings I experienced on anyone. But I found Jesus in those days in a way I had never experienced before. They were days that I encountered, intensely, the now and not yet of the Kingdom of God. The pain was so real. The anxiety was overwhelming. At times God felt so far away. But the love of the church was all-surrounding. The voice of Jesus had never been louder to me and my family. And the sense that Jesus was not going to let us go — that he was there in the room with us — was never more powerful. It was a painful, beautiful, tension. It was there I found my pastor.

Shalene has been cancer-free since the day the doctors operated and cut the melanoma from her skin. From a medical point of view, what remains is a four-inch scar and a life of visiting dermatologists and keeping a vigilant eye out for bothersome moles.

As mentioned, the diagnosis from the very beginning was positive. At one point we even had a doctor suggest that the biopsy could have been a mistake; perhaps there was never any cancer at all. Looking back now with a clearer mind I could easily suggest that maybe there never was anything to be worried about. Some have suggested just that. But that is not the point for Shalene and I. What happened to us, happened. And while I have never thought that God made it happen, I deeply believe that while it happened, he walked with us. No matter the medical science of it all, something divine took place through those weeks, months, and years.

We praise the God who is our healer.

Right around the time Shalene received the cancer diagnosis, she found out she was pregnant with our third child. All of the subsequent cancer care during those nine months complicated everything to do with the pregnancy. We had to have a meeting with the specialist where we were told that if the cancer spread to the baby, he or she would be born terminal and die soon after. None of that would be known until after the baby was born and the placenta could be biopsied. Then during the pregnancy we were informed that Shalene had placenta previa which meant that she would need to have a cesarean section. Another scar.

Any of these things on their own would have been enough, but they were all happening together. It was nine months of normal pregnancy emotions, complications, and then all of the emotions and darkness connected with cancer. It was a mess.

But on August 15, 2013, Shalene gave birth to a beautiful, healthy, baby boy. We named him Brit Phoenix. Brit is our version of the Hebrew word which means covenant or promise. Phoenix represents the ancient image of the great bird who died in flames but was fully restored to even greater beauty.

In sharing some of her journey with our church family in the days after all of this, Shalene wrote these words:

At times I have looked at these cancer scars, ugly and gross, and they have brought back the memories — the fear and the feeling of being abandoned all come flooding back. I have wanted to erase these scars and forget what happened. I have wanted to move on and not look back. But then the memories of experiencing God's love come rushing back, too. I remember lying on the operating table as doctors and nurses surrounded me ready to remove the cancer. I laid on that operating table trembling, still in disbelief that it was all happening. But as I lay on that hard operating table I saw Him. I saw Jesus. He was there, at the end of my bed, watching me, and watching the doctors, helping as they stitched me up. He was there looking out for me. I was so overcome with emotion and gratefulness because I was not alone. And as I remember those moments, I see these scars as beautiful — as a physical reflection of how God has proven his love for me and that he has not abandoned me.

Then I received my most recent scar. From this scar came the gift that confirms the promise of God's love. Brit Phoenix was born on August 15 via cesarean section. And now, when I hold him in the quiet still night, I sense God saying, "This. This is your hope. This is your promise. This is how I love you." Through my last scar God has shown the truth of his powerful love; that he can indeed raise up the phoenix from the ashes — that life can come after death.

So vivid in my head is the image of a loving mother cradling her baby. But I have not been the mom in this picture. I have been the baby. And God, he has been my mother. This has been profound for me. I didn't trust a father right now. All I could think of was that a Father might abandon me. But a mother - that was a picture I could rest in. I would not trade these scars for anything. It is through these scars that I have seen Jesus. It is through these scars that I have truly come to understand how much he loves me. I have experienced and felt his love. And it is overwhelmingly good.

We praise the God who is our healer.

Several months ago, at the direction of our son's paediatrician — the son who had epileptic seizures — we began the process of taking him off of his medication which kept the seizures at bay. Slowly, we lowered the dosage until just recently he was taken completely off the medication and now shows no signs of seizures or complications. While it is common for children to grow out of these types of seizures as they get older, that has not stopped us from reflecting on yet another area through which Jesus met us and ministered to us.

We praise the God who is our healer.

After almost a year of back and forth with the Canadian Revenue Agency, the matter of the money owing was settled. The case was solved and no debt was owed. I can almost laugh now at how ludicrous it was that this declared debt happened alongside everything else that was taking place in our life during those days. Absolutely ridiculous.

Especially during winter — the season in which I am now writing this conclusion — both Shalene and I still feel the effects of the deep depression and anxiety we experienced all those years ago. Like Shalene's scar that will never go away completely, we have triggers that can make the darkness rear its ugly head. We remember and can still feel the pain, but time is a healer, counselling is game-changer, medication can help, doctors that fight for you are invaluable, friends that stick by you are to be cherished, and God is the great teacher and healer who never misses an opportunity to reveal his good character to us. In God's love we have come so far. We remain in the process of being healed.

We praise the God who is our healer.

I give God thanks and praise for how these stories ended up. The point of these stories is not to suggest that all stories end well. I know that is not the case. The point of these stories is to highlight how God used them to give me a testimony of his presence that I never had before. These stories are about seeing how God is in the business of giving us tulips and rainbows, signs that he is with us, that he is present, and that his voice is for us to hear. These stories are about his love and his persistent wooing of us. These stories prompt us, and my stories always remind me that Jesus will pastor us, lead us, and guide us and our churches if we let him.

―――――

Our little church is now in its eighth year. Our leadership team had a retreat just a few weeks ago and we spent a few hours reminiscing about the early days and talking about the things that shaped our DNA. Some of those at the retreat were there for the first days and some have come since. As we told the stories to those who have joined us along the way, I was so blessed and encouraged.The darkness that Shalene and I went through shaped our church in its infancy. It made a beautiful space for anyone to ask questions, to doubt, and to not have it all together. When the pastor of the church — me — doubts his own faith in sermons and wonders aloud if any of this is even real, a church will either embrace that pastor and walk with them or, sadly, and perhaps more likely, fire them or hide them in a closet. I am so grateful that my church did the former. Their pubic display of care and compassion toward me set the groundwork for a church that welcomes anyone in any state. We all come as a people who need Jesus to be real. It was not the way I would have drawn up the first year of our church, but again, I would not change it for anything. We have become a great place for people looking for faith to be real while acknowledging real doubts and questions.

Our church has mostly grown numerically through procreation. We are a church of young families with kids and more coming in the proverbial ovens. This is the point of the book where I regretfully inform you that if you think any of what I have said or suggested will be the magic bullet to see people come to faith *en masse*, you will probably be disappointed. None of this is about church numerical growth, per se. But it is certainly about growth. We are a church of seventy people. In six years we have gone from a group of twenty-five to seventy, and like I said, the majority of that growth has come because of the birds and the bees. While I desire to see my friends and neighbours who have not joined the Jesus story get onboard and come to know him, I am also at peace about the way in which our church has been faithful to what God has asked us to do together and in our community. I am excited about the transformational steps we have all taken together toward Jesus and his kingdom. Part of this journey for me in discovering Jesus as our pastor has been learning to trust him in leading us into being faithful in our time and context. He will decide what that needs to look like. I am not trying to lead my church into chasing any dream of church numerical growth, more baptisms, more conversions, more money, or bigger and better programs. I am trying to model that life is about dying and living in Jesus. In that relationship, he will lead us, day to day, in the things he wants from us. I have no doubt that Jesus wants to see people come to faith in him and live their lives for the kingdom. But he will accomplish that through me and with me in his good way as I surrender myself to him and do the little things each day. While being a world changer or incredible leader makes for inspiring conference lectures, books, and cat poster slogans, and while every now and again a Billy Graham or Phoebe Palmer emerges, the vast majority of us have the beautiful opportunity to be obedient, Spirit-filled, followers of Jesus in small ways in our community *right now*. In 100 years most of us will be forgotten. But we will have served the eternal kingdom.

All of this is a risk. So much of what I have suggested is about giving up control or using what control or leadership you do have to model dependency on the Spirit. While any destination of a journey surrendered to Jesus is good, about redemption, and saturated in his love, it is unknown to us before we set sail. That is frightening. But on the other side of that risk, surrender, and acknowledgement of the real presence of Jesus and his desire to be for us and with us, is the realization that he really *is that* good — that he *will* move all things toward the full redemption of his creation. He cares about us. He cares about his church. He cares about our development as humans. He wins and we get to join him in the victory.

I do not have this all figured out. As of right now I am frustrated and struggling with some things in our church. I want to see more of Jesus. I want to see him doing more things in our midst. I want it now. I am comfortable being a part of a crazy group of people who believe Jesus can do some crazy things *even when we do not see those crazy things happen*. But that is a hard place to be for any length of time. It is faith and we all know that faith is not always easy. But my experience with Jesus as our pastor is that he is often teaching us the way in which we, in our context and time, need to learn and grow. As often as we make rules in our churches and denominations regarding how we will go about experiencing the presence of Jesus, Jesus comes and messes with them because he knows what we need. He knows what things we need to die to. He knows our hangups, doubts, and struggles. He knows our areas of pride. He knows that if it were as easy as "Just follow these four steps and then you will experience Jesus do _____" we would not pursue him and his voice. We would instead use him, manipulate him and each other, and consider ourselves saviours and masters. He will always help us know how to be a servant, how to depend on him, and that he is with us and is good. To receive his shepherding we must take the risk of surrender. We must submit to the pastor. We must lead our people into this submission. Like Jesus' parables of the treasure in the field and the pearl of great worth, the gift and value of living in the throws of God's kingdom is too much and too great not to give it all up to receive all of his goodness.[1]

I earlier described the items we have at the centre of our worship gathering on Sundays.[2] In the middle of it all stands that singular candle that we light in recognition of Jesus' presence with us. I am usually the person who blows it out after the service has been dismissed. People get up from their seats and the weekly tradition of talking, laughing, maybe continued praying, eating and finishing up cups of coffee begins. I admit that I always feel a slight discomfort when I blow out that candle. I am not trying to be too dramatic. I do not believe that I am extinguishing Jesus'

---

[1] Matthew 13:44-46
[2] See page 54

presence. The candle is a symbol. But it is a powerful one for me and our church. Every time I blow it out I am led to think about its significance in my life. I so desperately need the candle to burn. I have so much to be thankful for in my life. I am surrounded by an incredible wife, kids, family, church family, and community. I have lived a great life of privilege and opportunity. But I am lost without the meaning of what that burning candle represents. I need Jesus. I need his voice. I need his help to restore my brokenness and dismantle my shame. I need his love and power to keep on keeping on. I need his lordship. I need his friendship. For a split second when I extinguish the candle I sense in my gut the potential despair of my life without Jesus. Then I am quickly thankful that it is just a candle, and that Jesus is smiling at me as I continue the journey.

Allow me to finish with this challenge. In North America, as church leaders, we are quickly realizing that our churches are mostly being forgotten by the culture around us. While spirituality is cool, the church is not usually seen as the place to seek it out. While every now and again there are short-lived experiences of persecution (so small that in light of what our sisters and brothers experience in other parts of the world I hesitate to even use the word), there is mostly apathy towards us. Our churches contribute good things to our communities and I have no doubt that some people would miss our churches if our doors closed for good. Many people will listen to our stories and cheer on our charitable causes and even support them sometimes. Yet our capacity to help these people cross the line from "I like what you do as a church" to "Tell me more about Jesus" is lacking.

My conviction is that embracing our craziness — recognizing and living like Jesus really is alive *right now* — and then having our lives and churches reflect that reality is the best shot we have of inviting people into something worth their lives. No more Wal-Mart church. No more best-business practices to help us run more efficiently. No more believing that we can be the sort of leader capable of being so great that we can be the messiah. It is time to quit pastoring in so many of the ways we once thought necessary and vital. No more believing in signs and wonders on paper but being functional cessationists. The titles, the language, the mechanisms, the practices, and the processes in our church must create space for Jesus to be seen and heard. No more talking like he is not in the room with us. He is here. With us. For us. Speaking. Leading us into truth. While we and our churches walk into the battle against both the seen and the unseen, we must do so by following our pastor. He is who makes us us.

I dare you to embrace the failure of the human project. We have nothing without Jesus. I dare you to embrace your craziness. He is alive. Right now. I dare you to make the changes in your life and in your church. Welcome him as pastor. May your testimony be one of Jesus' voice and presence. And may you receive your flowers and see your rainbows.

Jesus is real.
He is with you.
He is for you.
He is your pastor.

Who is *New Leaf Network Press*?

Starting something new is hard, and when you are breaking new ground you often feel alone. In those moments of feeling alone, finding someone else who is on a similar journey is so important. Many of us have found those encouraging voices in books that we have read. Yet, in the publishing market of resources for the Canadian church, there is often a gap where distinctly Canadian stories and resources should be. That's where *New Leaf Network Press* comes in.

We are a small scale imprint committed to offering the work of Canadian authors to a Canadian audience. We are part of the *New Leaf Network*, and all of our publications seek to support the broader network.

The *New Leaf Network* is a collaborative, relational and creative missional organization that supports, equips and connects church planters, spiritual entrepreneurs and missional practitioners in post-Christian Canada.

**Whether you're starting from scratch
or leading an existing community,
we want to help you start something new
right here on Canadian soil.**

We've got a hunch that our ever-increasing post-Christian culture is begging for new forms of Jesus-centered cultural engagement, neighbourhood connection and mission innovation. We believe it's time for Canadian Jesus-followers to unite together, equip each other, cultivate our voice and start something new from coast-to-coast.

Through online collaboration spaces, interactive learning workshops, events, story-telling and specialized coaching, this growing collective of Canadian, Jesus-centred leaders is a community of innovators, both church and lay leaders, working to lead from the emerging future.

For more information visit

www.newleafnetwork.ca/newleafpress

www.ingramcontent.com/pod-product-compliance
Lightning Source LLC
Chambersburg PA
CBHW070422010526
44118CB00014B/1861